# Locked in the Psych Ward

# Locked in the Psych Ward

*A Memoir of Broken Promises and False Confessions*

Jamie Lyn Weaver

Weaving Words Press

# Dedication

*During the satanic panic era, countless lives were lost or,
like my own, irrevocably altered.*

*This book is dedicated to all the innocent people who, through no fault of their
own, became victims of misdiagnosis and mistreatment by unscrupulous
healthcare professionals.*

# Table of Contents

# Echoes of Panic

The year was 1985, and I—a naïve 39-year-old woman—was urgently in need of help. I was seeing things that weren't there, my marriage was crumbling, and my compulsive sexual behavior was out of control.

I had sought help from various therapists many times, but no one could get to the bottom of what was wrong with me. Finally, out of desperation, I made a cold call to a psychiatrist who, unknown to me at the time, was fixated on cults and satanic ritual abuse.

We met in his private office, and after a brief interview with Dr. Bennett G. Braun, I agreed to enter Rush Presbyterian Hospital in Chicago for a three-month evaluation. He promised me a diagnosis and treatment plan. But instead of getting the therapeutic help I was promised, this unethical psychiatrist admitted me to a psychiatric ward and overprescribed psychotropic drugs.

Although I didn't understand this at the time—and was so desperate for help that I didn't immediately question the treatment—there was no medical reason for these drugs. They didn't stop my compulsions or save my marriage; they only dulled my ability to process what was happening to me under his care. By the end of his career, this psychiatrist would be sued at least twelve times for wrongdoing. In 2020, he surrendered his license to prescribe controlled substances to avoid criminal prosecution.

Dr. Braun practiced in partnership with Dr. Roberta (Bobbi) G. Sachs, lacked the professional decorum and, by today's standards, also lacked the credentials to practice in a psych ward. Bobbi, even more than Braun, used incorrect and outdated forms of therapy to plant the false memories needed to keep me locked up long enough to convince me that I was a satanic-ritual-abuse survivor. I was "treated" only as long as my insurance money lasted. Four years later, when my benefits were nearing their end, Braun and Bobbi declared me well enough to be discharged. They offered no guidance on how to reenter the real world. I left that ward in far worse shape than when I went in. My life would be forever changed.

Writing this book has been on my mind for thirty-six years, but there was always an excuse not to start. Authoring a book felt daunting. I had a master's degree in library science, but no training as a writer. I had spent my high school years in remedial English, but I had read widely across many genres since I was old enough to hold a book. I worried my story was too intimate, too embarrassing, too macabre.

After a lot of spiritual work and soul-searching around forgiveness, I still had those concerns. Yet I knew the only chance I had to feel forgiven was to put my guilt and shame on the back burner and tell my story as I remembered it.

But reading and writing felt like two different things. Where to start?

In July 2020, a *How to Start My Memoir* opportunity was announced in an email. A company was offering a free week-long book-writing workshop. It felt too good to be true. COVID was in full swing, and I—like everyone else—was sheltering in place. I signed up, never dreaming that my life would change once again.

The workshop was helpful, and by the end of the week I had a list of one hundred moments I could turn into my book. Yes, they were only moments, but I knew they held the truth about what had happened. I would prioritize each one and, for the first time, take a hard look at what had been done to me.

The act of writing can be healing and can open doors to deeper insight. I wrote at my kitchen table in my tiny studio apartment while soft instrumental music played in the background. Somehow that allowed me to go deeper than I had ever gone. The melancholy sounds of violin and piano tugged at me, and I could feel the dam of resistance breaking apart.

I have heard many people say you shouldn't write your memoir until you've made peace with your trauma, but I can't entirely agree. Writing was the only way I could get close enough to the pent-up emotions I had never expressed. It was painful but, in the end, clarifying and rewarding.

As I researched Dr. Braun, mental health, the satanic panic era, and how drugs and therapies were misused on me, I could clearly see I wasn't responsible for what you will soon learn I did and said to keep my sanity. It didn't take long for me to realize I had been duped. After this revelation, most days I did my research and wrote until I wanted to destroy everything in sight. My anger was volatile. The only way I knew to lessen it was to let the cleansing tears fall while I paced the halls where I lived. Or I would go outside and scream, "Fuck you! Every damn one of you can rot in hell forever." I threw stones at the pavement until my voice was gone and my arms ached so badly, I had to stop. Calmer after my walks, I would start writing again. My days—and sometimes nights—were filled with remembering, reliving, and recording what I had experienced. It was brutal, but necessary work. My drafts were getting closer to the truth. And when I finally got to that truth, I was stunned by the severity of what had happened to me. It took my breath away.

What I experienced will always be part of who I am. I will always be slow to trust what people tell me, and I will panic when I feel I've been lied to or backed into a corner.

But only through the writing of this memoir have I begun to

find a measure of peace and acceptance. With each revelation of why and how I was manipulated, I have been able to loosen the noose of guilt and shame around my neck. That, in turn, has enabled me to come closer to the self-forgiveness I had hoped to find when I started this project.

I have come from self-blame to understanding that I dealt with self-aggrandizing physicians whose "therapy" was criminal. They preyed upon women like me, and I did the best I could under the circumstances I found myself in. For that truth and knowledge, I am profoundly grateful.

It is my sincere wish that by reading my story, you will ultimately be uplifted and see it as a call to question treatment, to get a second opinion, to research physicians and their practices—but most of all, to stand up for yourself in the face of oppressive treatment. Sadly, the medical profession, just like any other, has its share of bad actors. If you find yourself in a compromising situation, I hope you'll remember my story and take what you need from it to help you reclaim your full, beautiful, and unique sense of identity and self.

# Chapter 1

## *Walking a Fragile Line*

It was inevitable that I would find myself in the baby section of Kmart. And now that I was here, I was overwhelmed.

I let my eyes drift across the various shelves, taking in the colors, textures, and imagined smells of infancy. Then, very slowly, I took a bottle off a shelf. It was wrapped in colorful, polka-dotted cellophane. The package made my fingers tingle in anticipation. I wanted that bottle. I wanted to drink warm milk from it.

Then I looked at pacifiers.

How long had it been since I'd poured my heart out while being held in someone's safe arms? Months? No, more like years. My utter sense of self-loathing would not allow me to seek that luxury. If babies felt comfort while sucking on a pacifier, then my fretful mind told me I could do so too.

I had no idea there were so many kinds of pacifiers. I picked up one, then put it back. I finally chose one with a heart-shaped ring. My mind wavered.

What am I doing? I asked myself. I was thirty-nine and married to a man I'd never loved. That very morning, I couldn't do laundry because I was terrified of a man with gray pants and cement shoes who hung out in a dark corner of the basement.

The hallucinations had started months ago. I knew he couldn't be real, but he still scared the shit out of me.

He wasn't half as scary as my sexual compulsions. They started with an affair with my boss fifteen years earlier. When that ended, I promised myself I would not have another. But I would break that promise and get caught again. I then started exposing my body while driving. Later, it became a compelling desire to view porn magazines.

I started to avoid eye contact, scared that people could see *obsessed with sex* across my forehead. In desperation, I reached out for help. But every damn social worker and psychiatrist I saw danced around my embarrassing symptoms. One psychiatrist even laughed. He told me I might be obsessive-compulsive or manic, but with this or that drug, I would be fine. I was not fine. I had lost friendships, self-respect, and now I was in Kmart trying to return to childhood.

The feeling was deep and strong. If I started my life over again with a dad who didn't drink and a mom who wasn't mentally ill, I would have the tools to be a normal, outgoing, self-assured adult —one who could love someone and not have compulsive behaviors or ugly, unacceptable sexual problems that were never named.

This thought made no sense. No one can start over. What you're born into can't be changed. But I was contemplating suicide, and this cockamamie plan to start over was the only thing keeping me alive. It's only now, fifty years later, that I can see the whole picture. What happens next in my story is like my visit to Kmart—inevitable.

Small, silver-handled spoons caught my attention. They would be perfect to use when I ate my next bowl of Farina. The cereal had a nutty, oat smell and a texture that reminded me of baby food and my never-ending desire to start my life over. The life I had was crumbling before my eyes. Quickly, those two packages joined the other items in my cart, and I headed to the checkout.

My route took me past the toy section, where I saw rows of

yellow boxes with the words *Cabbage Patch Kids* inscribed within grass-green cabbage leaves. Nestled in each set of leaves was the head of a bald, blue-eyed baby. Each box read, "I'm unique. I'm adoptable."

All thoughts of checking out vanished as my jaw dropped and my eyes opened wide. These dolls are so cute, I thought. I need one. Right? Yep, you do, my mind said. They sure look like something you could cuddle and tell your troubles to.

Each "kid" seemed to be saying, pick me. No, pick me. No, pick me. I wanted a girl, and after looking at each face, hair color, and style at least four times, I chose one with big blue eyes and brown pigtails. She wore a white dress with tiny pink roses and had a pink birth certificate tied to her wrist. She was perfect, and she joined the other items in my cart.

Once home, I stared at my new "adoptee" through the transparent plastic. Part of me wanted to rip the box open immediately, while at the same time another part was terrified that I'd be opening the proverbial Pandora's box. If I took her out and held her, would I finally cross the fragile line between staying in the adult world or fully giving in to the obsession of reentering a child's?

I'd read in my psychology textbook that Carl Jung believed we all had an inner child. But for a long time now, my inner child felt like she wanted to escape and be known.

Opening the rest of my packages seemed like a safer thing to do. Carefully, I freed my new purchases and placed them on the counter next to my crusted Farina bowl. I conscientiously washed everything with Ivory soap and hot water. Then I hid the items in my underwear drawer.

Hiding stuff was now normal for me. My last affair—with my best friend's husband—had put a crater bigger than Alaska between my husband, Dave, and me. We avoided one another as much as possible. All trust was gone, and I had no idea if he was still looking for further evidence of my unfaithfulness.

Still, I felt like a small child hiding the evidence of a crime because they didn't want to 'fess up to what they'd done. No, I did not want to 'fess up that I bought baby items because I wanted to use them.

I held out until after a silent dinner with Dave. I shut the door of my office bedroom, initially intended to be used for our first child. It was now a hangout for our dog, Penny, and my place to pay bills.

My heart fluttered as I saw the doll's blue eyes staring at me. "Hold on, little one," I said. "You'll be out of that old box soon. I can't wait to hold you." Once freed from the long plastic twist ties that held her in place, my face lit up. "You fit perfectly in my arms!" Hot tears blurred my vision as I kissed the top of her curly, chestnut-brown hair. She was so damn cute. Exploring the rest of her body, I laughed when I discovered she had a round belly button and a squiggly signature on her bottom.

Over the next few weeks, I created a new routine for myself. After Dave left for work, I'd have a breakfast of cereal or soft-boiled eggs spooned into my mouth using my silver-handled spoons. Then I'd change the doll's store-bought preemie diaper and put her in a new outfit with different-colored hair ribbons. I'd spent hours compulsively buying and then cutting the thin satin to the right length. I even bought her pink, ruffled rubber pants.

My next task was to pull out the half-finished résumé from my desk and start to put my job skills down on paper. I had a newly awarded bachelor's degree in education. I had worked as a classroom assistant, but I had no faith in my ability to teach. Soon, letters would swim on the page, and I'd place all my scribbles back in the drawer and promise myself I'd get it all done tomorrow.

This routine helped some, but even with my doll, my yearning to return to childhood was escalating. My world was growing smaller, while my anxiety level and need for sexual outlets grew larger. I had no friends I could call. I spoke less but read more of my childhood *Little Golden Books* while eating peanut butter and jelly sandwiches cut into toddler bite-sized pieces.

The other thing I couldn't ignore was the compulsive draw of the small playground near my home. When I was little, the swings in our backyard comforted me. On many days when Mom had been on the warpath—pretending to call the orphanage to come get my brother and me or pulling out the gray-green army belt with the shiny buckle that flashed danger—I'd head to my backyard. There, the swing would help me breathe as I pumped my little legs and let go of my swirling fears and anger. I'd make up songs and sing until every bit of worry left my body.

This playground wasn't pretty, but it provided me with a space that lent itself to childlike behavior. I could sing nursery rhymes, skip, or dig my hands into the nasty gravel if I wanted to. I felt invisible because even when moms brought their kids for a playdate, nobody seemed to give a damn that I was there.

A few oak trees gave shade to two uneven swings with cracked black seats. Each rusty chain left orange stains on the palms of my hands. They squeaked like steel doors badly in need of oil. After my swing, I'd head for the dayglo orange slide and climb to the top. There I would sit for the rest of the day and dream as I watched the clouds change shapes.

It was on one of those cloud-watching days that I heard a child's voice. "Hey, lady, whatcha doing up there? I wanna go down the slide."

Lady? I didn't feel like any lady I knew. No grown-up "lady" could be this close to shattering into a million pieces or feel this abandoned and alone.

Is this some kind of wake-up call? I thought. This kid was right. What was I doing up here—and with my life? I'd destroyed my marriage. Dave was now a stranger. He needed to be set free. Hell, I needed to be set free soon, or I would die.

So many things were wrong. I had no job, and my compulsive behavior ran rampant. My doll had more clothes than I did. I fed myself with baby spoons and used the bottle and pacifier for comfort. Nothing soothed. Nothing was enough. All my efforts to start over only made me feel more out of control and scared that I was headed down the same road as my mother.

Mom developed postpartum depression after I was born. This eventually turned into postpartum psychosis, which worsened after each of my two brothers was born. Like me, she saw things that weren't there and was never the same mom two days in a row. She finally needed electroshock therapy and was now having a hard time remembering I was her daughter. She'd retreated into a world of her own made-up fantasies—my worst fear.

As I slid down the slide, tears ran down my face. "Sorry," I said to the boy. "It's your turn. Have fun."

I took the long way home, kicking stones and, just like when I walked to grade school, I avoided stepping on cracks because, as the rhyme went, I'd break my mother's back. So many childhood behaviors were returning. It's time to make that call I've put off for so long, I said to myself. I need help before I self-destruct.

# Chapter 2

## *My Fate is Sealed*

I dialed. The phone rang, and the prerecorded voice said, "You have reached the office of Dr. Bennett G. Braun. Please leave a message."

"Hello, my name is Linda Cooper, and I'd like to make an appointment with Dr. Braun as soon as possible. My phone number is…" That's all I could manage to say. With shaky hands, I replaced the receiver, having no idea that I was on my way to a hell I never thought possible.

Our home was on one of the primary flight paths for O'Hare International Airport. As I waited for a return phone call from this new potential psychiatrist, I watched a plane fly across the cloudless sky. Would this plane explode and fill the sky with falling suitcases and bodies? Probably not, I thought. I had counted six planes by the time the phone rang. None exploded. They never do, even when somewhere within my anxious mind I'm sure they will.

When the phone rang, my birthdate, marital status, and insurance information secured the first open appointment. I would be seeing a Dr. Braun on Monday, August 26, at 2 p.m. It was 1985.

While standing in front of the mirror, drying my newly cut

bob with its thin strands of platinum highlights, I wondered what I should wear to see this psychiatrist. Casual, business, sexy? My body wanted to wear sexy clothes, as it was a muggy day and my sexual compulsions remained heightened in hot weather.

I dug through my dresser drawer and pushed the baby bottle aside. Then I dressed in no-frills white Carter's underwear and a green cotton shirtwaist. People always said that dress made my green eyes sparkle. Hopefully, this psychiatrist would keep his eyes on mine and not wander to places where they didn't belong.

Recently, when I drove, I would hear cars crashing into each other. Just like with the planes, there were no actual accidents. Even so, the thought of driving in city traffic overwhelmed me. I decided to take the train.

I knew nothing about this doctor I was supposed to see. Maybe, I thought, I should leave and think this through a bit more. But before I could turn around, the inner office door opened.

"Hi, Mrs. Cooper, I'm Dr. Braun. You're right on time. My office is in here," he said with a smile that didn't quite feel genuine.

Breathe, I told myself.

He appeared to be in his mid-forties. Large, round glasses highlighted his receding hairline. He wore a crisp white dress shirt with buttons straining across his broad frame, a burgundy tie, and black pants.

"Have a seat." He sat in his chair behind an oversized mahogany desk that, for a doctor, looked relatively well organized.

"So, what brings you here?" he asked, picking up a gold pen and opening an empty folder with my name on it. "I see by your birthdate that you're thirty-nine."

I nodded yes.

"Married?" he asked, glancing at my twisting fingers.

"Yes. We had our thirteenth anniversary last week. And, well, I'm here because my marriage is falling apart, and I do things I don't understand."

"Children?" he asked.

"No," I said as my eyes scanned his desk for the usual silver-framed photo of a wife, kids, and family dog. There was none.

"So, what kind of things don't you understand?" His gold pen flashed, making notes.

"I started seeing things about two years ago. I was reading at home when suddenly I saw a little girl, about four years old. She looked just like me at that age. She was dressed in pink pajamas and—well, um—she could talk, or we could talk, or… I don't know," I said, shifting in my chair and blowing out an exasperated breath.

This was harder to admit than I thought. Deep down, I was afraid that if I told anyone what I was seeing and hearing, they would think I was crazy. Still, oddly enough, it felt good to finally share this openly. If I couldn't be honest with this doctor, then I had no hope of ever getting answers. This was my last-ditch effort.

"All I know is she felt real, and I named her Noel because I was born three days before Christmas. She stayed around for about a month before she kind of disappeared, and I don't see her anymore."

His eyebrows raised. "Interesting," he said while taking more notes. "Do you see anything else?"

"Umm," I said, biting my lip. "Yes. It started again around six, maybe seven, months ago. I see the bottom half of a man in my basement. He has gray pants and cement shoes. I know he's not there, but. …"

This sounded crazy, even to me. But I had already put my sanity on the line by admitting to seeing Noel, so I stopped mid-sentence and hurriedly said, "And recently I bought this Cabbage Patch doll and a baby bottle and then go to a playground near my home and swing and sit on top of the slide." I let out a brief sigh of relief and trepidation that this compulsive behavior was also out.

Dr. Braun remained expressionless as he sat in his office chair, watching me struggle to push back tears.

"Do you know why you do this?" he asked.

"No," I said, staring at the floor. "I don't know why I do anything."

He had a few more questions that I don't remember. I was on overload and couldn't answer any more.

"I think I have enough information for now," he said. "From what you're telling me, I believe you could benefit from a three-month evaluation at Rush Presbyterian Hospital. We would observe, run tests, and ask questions. In the end, you will have a diagnosis and a treatment plan. How does that sound?"

The room began to swim. "Three months? That's kind of a long time, isn't it?"

"Do you want answers? I thought that's why you came," he said in an overly loud voice that made me feel wrong to question his suggestion.

Anger churned inside as the doctor spoke. His voice turned into my mother's as I heard her say, "Be a good girl and do what you're told." My stomach burned like hot liquid about to erupt like a volcano. I was afraid of that feeling. I might hurl whatever my fingers touched across the room or say hurtful things.

Shit, I thought. I desperately need answers, but every call for help I'd ever made had never led to any cure for my obsessions or compulsions. Instead, the drugs I received ate away at my self-esteem.

My mind was jumbled. It was so very hard to think.

"Now, if you agree, I can make a quick call and see when we can get you in," he said.

I couldn't decide if this was the right choice. I'd run out of options and wasn't sure how long I could stay in the adult world. But I also knew that when I got this mixed up, I'd gone past the point of thinking clearly.

From somewhere beyond my rational mind, I heard myself say, "OK, I'll do it."

As Dr. Braun left the room to make his call, I took several deep breaths and distracted myself by studying the framed diplomas on the wall. He graduated from the University of Illinois in 1968, was on staff at Rush, and was board-certified in psychiatry. For the first time, I noticed a window behind this doctor's desk. Shafts of sunlight crossed it, illuminating a myriad of dancing dust motes that, for some reason, brought me childlike delight.

"All set," he said when he returned.

I wasn't "all set" in any way, shape, or form. How was I going to explain this decision to my family?

But it was easier to explain to Dave why I was going to check myself into a hospital than to tell my parents.

"I saw a new doctor today," I said after a dinner of leftovers.

With a surprised look on his face, he said, "Oh?"

"It's just that I feel like I'm becoming more like my mother every day, and, well, I don't want to end up like her with electric shock treatments. This doctor is confident that I will receive a diagnosis and a treatment plan if I agree to a three-month stay at Rush Presbyterian. I think I need to try."

I saw a moment of relief pass over his face. "When would you go?"

"Next Tuesday, the day after Labor Day."

All he said was, "I think this will be good."

My parents did not understand. Still, I knew they had no idea what was really happening with their daughter. I could hide my feelings faster and more deeply than a squirrel could bury its nuts. All my dad knew was that I was about to go to the same hospital where my mom had electric shock treatments that left her in a constant state of confusion. And he didn't want me to go.

I changed my mind about going to the hospital at least twice a day. I didn't trust psychiatrists. Not one helped my mother or me. Dr. Braun might be a good psychiatrist, I told myself, but his mannerisms made me feel very uncomfortable.

I wasn't worried about leaving Dave, my home, or my current life, but I was worried about leaving my dog Penny. She was my life. She seemed to sense something was wrong, and since I couldn't sleep, I pulled her into my lap for a last cuddle. "It's only for three months," I whispered in her ear. "You'll be fine without me. You know you're my bestest girl ever, don't you? Plus, you're the only one I'm able to love." She snuggled close, and as I held her warm body against my heart, I filled her fur with tears.

The rest of the night was spent quietly walking around the moonlit house, touching various items and thinking about where they came from and what they meant to me. When dawn arrived, I slipped into a pair of faded jeans, pulled a T-shirt from the Wisconsin Dells over my head, grabbed my brown sweater, and went out to the playground for one last swing.

I returned home before Dave was up and, for the first time in many moons, made us both a breakfast of bacon and eggs. It felt like the least I could do.

I needed to check in by 11, so allowing for traffic jams, Dave and I left around 9:30. We briefly discussed the weather, and I mentioned that Penny had a vet visit coming up. Then we fell into silence, letting the car radio fill our thoughts.

We pulled into the driveway of a tall redbrick building that signaled we were at the Kellogg Pavilion.

"Do you want me to come in with you?"

"No. Thanks. I need to do this on my own. I'll call when I know more."

I wish I could say, *I'm sorry for all I've put you through. I know everything will turn out OK for us.* But I knew I couldn't tell him that. Yes, I was sorry for what I had done to Dave, to us. But I had no idea if I would be OK. I also knew that no matter the outcome of this hospitalization, I still wanted out of this marriage.

"OK," he said, setting my suitcase on the sidewalk.

I sensed him come closer for a goodbye kiss. I pulled away, unable to find any comfort or kindness. I saw an anguished look cross Dave's face. I had hurt him again. It seemed that's all I ever did. It was time to find out why.

# Chapter 3

## *No Way Out*

Sweat trickled down my spine as I watched Dave's car drive away. "Hey, God," I shouted to the overcast sky, "are you sure this is the right thing for me to do? Kellogg Pavilion sounds more like a place where I can buy my Farina than a hospital. If you're up there somewhere, please watch over me, OK?"

I stood tall, grabbed the strap of my red suitcase, slung my purse over my shoulder, and headed into the place I hoped would bring answers.

Admissions was on the first floor. Still scared, I wrapped my walnut-brown cardigan sweater—my adult "blankie"—tightly around my body. Then I looked for the lady with the kindest face and made my way to her cubicle.

"Name, please?"

"Cooper, Linda. I… I, uh, was supposed to check in by 11 a.m."

"Let's see what we have here," she said with a smile. "It looks like you're right on time and are being admitted to the psychiatric ward on the thirteenth floor. Are you admitting yourself of your own free will?"

A gasp escaped me as bile rose in my throat. This was surprising. I genuinely believed I would be admitted to a general unit for this evaluation, not to some nutcase ward. Wasn't number thirteen bad luck?

I held my breath and curled my fingers into tight fists as my mind frantically tried to remember if the words *psychiatric ward* were ever mentioned during my meeting with Dr. Braun. I'd remember that, right? I knew we discussed my compulsions and my doll, but I couldn't recall being told where my evaluation would take place in the hospital.

I felt rattled to my core. My body quivered like a bowl of Jell-O as I argued with myself. Linda, you could refuse to sign and walk out. But then what? You were promised a diagnosis and treatment plan by a well-known doctor. You can't back out now. This is your last chance to find out what's wrong with you. You've come this far. You can do this. When you leave here, you will be a brand-new, confident woman in charge of your life.

"Mrs. Cooper, are you OK?"

Slowly, I nodded yes, as tears welled and the words *like mother, like daughter* washed over me. The woman calmly asked again, "Are you admitting yourself of your own free will?"

"Shit, I guess," I mumbled as I wiped away tears and wondered if I looked as conflicted as I felt.

"Once you've filled out the information on these forms to the best of your ability, you will need to sign with an X to verify self-admittance."

It didn't take long to fill out and check the boxes, but it was long enough to cause so much anxiety that my signature looked more like a 3-year-old's than a woman of 39. All I could say was, "Sorry. This is the best I can do."

She held up a long white plastic hospital bracelet, then managed another smile and asked for my hand. This is it, I thought as she pulled it tight around my wrist and snipped off the excess. I am now officially cut off from the world I know.

"Please have a seat under the picture of sunflowers. A staff member will be down to escort you to the ward."

I couldn't sit still, so like *The Little Engine That Could*, I paced the floor and kept repeating, "I think I can, I think I can." When that didn't soothe me, I picked up a magazine. Still unable to concentrate, I let my fingers play with my too-tight hospital bracelet while I watched a mother play peekaboo with her copper-haired toddler.

How I longed to cover my eyes and go back to a different time and place. But before I could wonder if anyone would miss me if I disappeared, someone called my name. I saw a woman with permed, mousy-brown hair, dressed in wide-legged tan slacks with a tan blazer and a candy-striped blouse, heading my way.

"My name is Kate. We've been expecting you."

I followed her like a lost puppy needing guidance home. We had the elevator to ourselves. Floor thirteen pinged. We stepped into a long, narrow, dimly lit entry that led to a windowless metal door. There were no pictures on the walls, no chairs to sit in, and no signs of welcome anywhere.

Kate pressed some buttons. The door opened. We walked through. Momentarily frozen, I waited until I heard the door clang shut behind me. The sound echoed through my body, setting every nerve on fire. It was then that I fully understood I was locked in. God! I screamed inside. What the hell have I done?

Like my mind and family life, the ward felt messy and chaotic. As I walked down a wide, brightly lit corridor, my eyes burned from the smell of bleach combined with cigarette smoke.

I made a face. Kate noticed. "Sorry. After lunch, patients can smoke if they want. Do you smoke?"

"No," I said, as my stomach cramped.

"Code yellow," a voice blared through an intercom. "Code yellow."

Startled, I stopped in my tracks. Kate said in a calm voice, "No worries. The staff knows what to do. You're safe." Apparently, this code was related to a spill, because two attendants appeared out of nowhere with mops and buckets.

"Here we are," she said in a sing-song voice. "Please put your suitcase and purse on the bed by the window. You'll be in room 1302 for now. Your roommate, Mary, is probably still at lunch."

Roommate?

My eyes traveled from her unmade bed to the floor, where a pair of jeans that looked around a size three, along with a tiny pair of thong underwear and a black tank top, were left in a crumpled heap. A can of Coke, a pack of cigarettes, and an unopened bag of chips sat on her table.

When Kate started to unzip my suitcase, I pulled my eyes away from Mary's side of the room and quickly grabbed my Cabbage Patch doll I'd stuffed in at the last minute.

"This won't take long. I need to remove any hazardous items, like this plastic bag your doll's clothes are in." I wasn't ready to explain why I had them, so I stayed silent. At the same time, I watched as scissors, nail clippers, curling iron, safety razor, blow-dryer, knitting needles, a belt from my bathrobe, the one around my waist, and laces from my sneakers, along with a mirror from my purse, were placed in a plastic tub with "Cooper" written on tape across the front.

"When you need any of these items, you can request them from the nurses' station. Your purse and any pills or valuables will be locked in this top drawer of your dresser," Kate said as she pulled a small set of keys out of her pocket. "I'm your nurse," she said with authority, "and I'll be your main contact on most days. Our shifts do change, so you might have someone new on any given day. I'll leave you to put your things away and check back later. Do you have any questions?"

I shook my head no. Panic had arrived and stolen my words. The morning check-in, the search of my suitcase, and the removal of my personal items finalized my inability to cope.

My room had puke-green walls and a scratched brown floor. Two standard hospital beds on wheels with matching vanities were on each side of the 300-square-foot room. A small, chipped sink and mirror stood in the corner by the door. Each patient had a three-drawer dresser and a rollaway hospital table with a large tissue box. The tiny bathroom barely contained a toilet and a small shower stall. A cross I wanted to rip off the wall hung high above each bed.

With my doll tucked under my left arm, I used my right hand to put my clothes away in the dresser drawers. I placed my empty journal, *The World of Pooh*, the doll's clothes, ribbons, preemie Pampers, and her new pink shoes in the vanity. I shut the drawer. Now what was I supposed to do?

Mary, the roommate, entered briefly. "What's your name?" she asked. All I could do was stare at the emaciated ghost of a young girl. I could guess why she was on the psych floor. I didn't answer.

"Take a picture, honey. It lasts longer," she said as she shrugged her shoulders. "I'm just here for my pack of ciggies. Toodles."

Overwhelmed, I retrieved my new notebook and pen from the vanity and made my first entry.

*September 5, 1985*

*This place is NOT what I signed up for. I feel like I'm surrounded by people like Mom. I wonder if she had her electric shock treatments on this floor. I never thought to ask Dad because I had enough of my own shit to deal with. But now I wish I had!*

A tap on the door interrupted my next thoughts. "Hi, I'm from the kitchen. Would you like some lunch? You must be hungry."

I shook my head no.

"Are you sure?"

My head bobbed up and down.

"Well, if you don't want lunch, then," she said through tight lips, "here's your menu for tonight's meal and the rest of the week. Please fill it out now."

I could feel my anxiety level rise, as well as my need to be in control. In a moment of rebelliousness, I sat on my hands and said, "I'll fill out my menu when I'm ready, not when I'm told."

Frustrated, the kitchen lady left the required sheet on my table and quietly left my room.

After that, various staff members peeked in, but no one asked me questions until I heard a soft voice at my door say, "Hello? Can I come in?"

"Hi, Linda. My name is Victoria, but I go by Vicki. I'll be your evening nurse and the one coordinating your care. I understand you're overwhelmed and haven't had lunch, but you do need to eat. How about dinner? I'll get us some soup and crackers, and we can have a light meal together."

I wasn't sure about this petite, middle-aged nurse whose large eyes matched her short brown hair, but soup sounded manageable since my breakfast of bacon and eggs was a distant memory. When she returned with a tray from the kitchen, she said, "We may be disturbed. Mary will be discharged tonight. You'll be without a roommate for a few days."

That's the best news I've heard all day, I thought.

The chicken soup was watery and difficult to eat with a small plastic spoon. A hard roll had been substituted for crackers. There was a pat of butter but no knife.

"Knives aren't allowed on the ward. You can use the handle of your spoon if you want."

I tried but got frustrated when the melted butter fell off the handle. Chocolate pudding was dessert. I used the same spoon with the buttery handle that now seemed to be an all-purpose utensil.

"Would you like to see the ward?" Vicki asked.

I nodded yes, grabbed my doll, and headed toward the door. I could see by Vicki's narrowed eyes and pursed lips that she didn't want me to take the doll but didn't make a big deal out of it.

"This floor is for general psych patients. Dr. Braun and his partner, Dr. Roberta Sachs, only see and work with the patients they admit. Here," she pointed lightly, "is where you will ask for your personal stuff, and over here is where you'll eat your meals." I poked my head in, but the smell of onions and grease was too overwhelming for me to stay more than a few seconds.

"Over here is where board games and family visits occur, and here is the TV room." Neither room held any appeal, so we moved on.

"I think that's all for now. Let's get you back so you can wind down. Questions?"

I shook my head no.

When I got back to my room, Mary was gone. Her bed was stripped. Only her box of tissues and the unopened bag of chips remained. I set the doll on the bed, sighed in relief, and reluctantly took off my sweater. The room blurred. I'd been almost 48 hours without sleep, and I couldn't handle another new experience. I knew it was too early to go to bed, but I didn't care. I closed my door, put on my PJs, and then dressed the doll in hers.

I let the tears flow as I pulled the curtains shut and climbed into a hard bed with a lumpy pillow. Out of habit, I made a space for Penny. I already missed her kisses and soft fur. I also missed my freedom. Three months felt like an eternity.

Yet, as my exhausted body slowly calmed down, there was a strange sense of relief. I didn't have to plan meals or wash clothes while worrying about the man in the basement who wasn't there. I didn't have to make conversation with people I disliked or check in with my mother. But most of all, I didn't have to pretend I loved Dave or try, try, try to fit into a world where I felt I didn't belong.

When I eventually ran out of tears, I blew my nose and tentatively stuck my thumb in my mouth for the first time. It felt soothing. Finally, I curled into a fetal position, ready to let my body sink into the deep abyss of dreamless sleep.

"Sorry, Mrs. Cooper, all patients' doors need to stay open," a voice whispered. "After 9 p.m., we do hourly rounds to ensure you're safe."

"Swell," I mumbled.

I woke up my first morning to the deep voice of a phlebotomist asking for my arm. It felt like a rude awakening, but that would become my hospital day: one rude awakening after another. When he was done, I glanced at my watch. It was 6:35 a.m.

I opened the curtains and took in my bird's-eye view of my new surroundings. There wasn't much to see except the backs of buildings and a few tiny patches of grass with sidewalks that didn't seem to lead anywhere.

I thought a shower might help me feel like it was a normal day in the real world. So, I grabbed my small plastic bottle of lavender-scented body wash and stepped into the shower. The semi-warm water helped a little, but nothing could wash away the fact that I was in a place full of uncertainties and had no control over what I might face.

As the ward started to wake up, curiosity took over me. With my doll under my arm, I stood in the doorway to see what was going on. There wasn't much to see, but I could smell fresh-brewed coffee. How could I get a cup?

While I was wondering, a staff member dressed in casual wear pushed a noisy medicine cart past my door and greeted me with a cheery, "Good morning—meds are given at 9 a.m. down by the nurses' station. See you there."

All thoughts of coffee vanished from my mind. "I hope she's wrong," I said to the doll. "I've been on meds before. All they did was make me feel loopy, and besides, they never cured a damn thing."

Soon, I became aware of the floor intercom calling out doctors' names and codes I didn't understand. The intercom seemed to work like an alarm clock, because I saw patients emerging from their rooms. Most were still in their nightclothes and looked like they were heading for the nurses' station to get their "hazardous" items—or the cup of coffee I still wanted but was too afraid to search for. I wasn't used to so many people. They ranged from teens to older adults. Some looked lost. One man, like me, was in conversation with an imaginary friend. He stood out. Did I stand out, too?

Quickly, I retreated into my room as my breakfast tray arrived.

I needed space, so I partially closed my door, happy to be alone. I stared at the tray. Nothing looked appealing. I wanted my baby spoon and a warm bowl of Farina. But at last, I did have my coffee.

After I pushed my half-eaten meal aside and drank the last of the bitter liquid, I pulled out my journal. It was time to make my first entry of the day. I was sitting in the middle of my bed, writing about the night rounds that were done with an annoying flashlight, when Dr. Braun appeared in the doorway. At first, I didn't recognize him. It took me a minute to realize the man I saw dressed casually in the office was the same man walking toward me in a white lab coat with the Rush logo.

I quickly shoved my pen into the journal pages, moved my table to the end of the bed, and grabbed my doll. With a few quick pushes, my body hit the low headboard that held my pillow in place. I pulled my knees up to my chin and automatically stuck my thumb in my mouth. I felt this urge to make myself small and disappear when I heard the metal door clang shut, and I didn't understand why the same sense of dread was here again.

Hesitantly, Dr. Braun pulled up a chair and, as he sat down, said, "Good morning, Linda. I'm Dr. Braun. Do you remember me?"

I nodded yes.

"Dr. Sachs will be joining us shortly. How are you today?"

The silence felt endless when a tall woman with broad shoulders entered the room, dressed in a black fringed top and flowing black skirt. She didn't resemble any doctor I'd ever seen, as she wore no lab coat. This made me realize that only Dr. Braun seemed to wear hospital attire in this ward.

Her short, professionally styled ash-blond hair framed her face, making her blue eyes shine when she smiled. She felt larger than life, and over time, she would prove to be just as addictive for me as baby bottles, pacifiers, naked car rides, and porn magazines.

Her eyes flicked to Dr. Braun, then over to me. I kept my gaze fixed on her as she crossed the room, pulled the other chair next to Dr. Braun, and sat down.

"You're safe here," she said, flashing me a smile that instantly lit up the corners of my heart.

She hesitated briefly before getting up from the chair. I felt like I had just been caught in a spider's sticky web. As I watched her silky black skirt glide across the white bedspread, my heart fluttered. I realized then that there was no escape. Suddenly, I caught the scent of Soir de Paris perfume. In that moment, I was back in my high school art room with my beloved art teacher. She also wore Soir de Paris. Who was this woman who ignited my mind and body?

"You can trust me, little one. Can you come closer, please?" she asked as her outstretched hand reached toward my curled-up body. "We need to get to know each other."

I tried to find words for what I was feeling but couldn't. I was smitten with this doctor who wore expensive designer clothes. I was confused by my behavior but not surprised when I slowly moved toward the hand I wanted to hold. You can't do that, my mind said, so I stopped just out of reach, adjusted the doll, and put my thumb back in my mouth.

Dr. Sachs smiled at me again. "Hi, sweetie. I'm Dr. Bobbi, and I'm here to help you get well. Can you tell me who's here?"

"Who's here?" I had no idea what she was talking about.

When there was no answer, she continued. "That's a lovely doll you have there. Does she have a name?"

"I don't like names," I muttered as I closed my eyes. A name? Why would I give her one? At events, I couldn't say my name. Names made things real. Names hurt people. My father called me "Pin." It made me feel small and insignificant. My mother called me "abnormal." My teachers called me "uncooperative." My body called me "stubborn, compulsive, addictive." So, no, I hadn't named my doll. Yet I felt compelled to answer her question, so slowly, I opened my eyes, removed my thumb, and quietly said the first name that came to my jumbled mind.

"Her name is Baby."

"May I hold her?" she asked.

Hesitantly, I handed her over.

"Well, Baby," Dr. Bobbi said as she cradled her in her arms, "you're very pretty, and I want all of you to know that I'm going to help you get well."

I watched silently, utterly fascinated, as she got off my bed, sat back in the chair, and introduced Baby to Dr. Braun. He played along, but the frown on his face never left. As Dr. Bobbi handed her back to me and her intense blue eyes met my green ones, I knew our bond was complete.

"I'll leave you now," she said, "but I'll see you tomorrow. Is that OK?"

I nodded yes.

"And I expect you to fill out your menu and eat your meals for me. Your meals can be in your room until you feel safer on the ward. OK?"

Again, I nodded in agreement. I would have agreed to scrub the floors with a toothbrush if she'd asked me to.

Dr. Braun said, "I need to leave, too. One of your nurses will be in later to start your psychological testing. Expect to receive a pill at 5 p.m."

"Well, Baby," I said after they both left, "I have no idea what just happened, but you have a name, and I gotta eat this crappy hospital food."

Vicki came in after lunch. She knew I wasn't adjusting well and started with nonthreatening questions. Soon, my words went from yes and no to, "Yes, I have a college degree. And no, I have no idea what's wrong with me."

It was nearly 5 p.m. when the test was completed, and as promised, Vicki handed me my first small white pill cup. I had no idea what I was about to take, so I stuck my tongue out in protest and then swallowed it with the necessary glass of water.

"There will be another at bedtime."

"Why?" I asked.

"It's doctor's orders." And with that, she walked out of my room. I picked up my journal.

*September 6, 1985*

*What the hell kind of answer is "It's doctor's orders"? I don't understand.*

*This feels off. How can I be diagnosed properly with meds in my system? I've only had one silly test that was just a bunch of lame questions. Did I mess up again? This place scares the hell out of me, and so does Dr. Bobbi. God, she's gorgeous. But she's also one of my doctors, so stop it, Linda. In three months, I'll get answers. Now it's time for bed.*

It was just past 9 p.m. when Dr. Bobbi appeared in my room. Baby and I were in PJs.

"Hi, cutie," she said. "I thought I'd stop by to say good night. How's Baby?" she asked with that smile that made my heart skip a beat.

"She's in her jammas," I whispered in a child's voice I didn't recognize as my own.

"I can see that. Sleep well, you two. I'll see you tomorrow."

# Chapter 4

## *Will You Marry Me?*

I was 20 and still living at home with my parents when I started to work for an insurance firm. My cubicle was tucked in the back corner, so I had an unobstructed view of the entire office. I'd just put a policy on my supervisor's desk when I spotted a new employee. I did a double take. He didn't look like any of the older guys I worked with. Most of them sported beer bellies, talked nonstop about what they did on weekends, and told off-color jokes when they thought I wasn't listening. This guy, however, was a bit taller than me and around my age. He had neatly combed brown hair, a broad forehead, and no glasses.

He was introduced as David Cooper, the new field agent. "Pleased to meet you," he told my supervisor and shook his hand. As his manager moved him along, he smiled my way and said, "I go by Dave." Hmm, not bad, I thought as my eyes followed him to the next department. This was new for me. I'd only had two short-term boyfriends. I ended both relationships when the boys tried to kiss me.

Dating and boys made me uncomfortable. Other girls seemed to enjoy the company of guys their age. I observed how easily they flirted with each other, held hands, and accepted hugs and even kisses. These kisses, they told me, were heavenly and expected on a date. I, however, had three rules. Always be polite. Don't share details of home life. And no kissing.

My friend and coworker, Martha, was one of those girls who liked kissing. She was also confident, outgoing, and knew about everyone's lives. One day, she told me, "You know you're not the only one who still lives at home with their parents. Dave, the new guy, does too. I think you should get to know him. He seems laid back, kind, and an all-around nice guy."

This was not the first time Martha had tried to set me up with someone. She had a steady boyfriend and was certain I needed one too. I always refused. I'd been set up with a guy for my senior prom and hated every second of his sweaty hands holding mine as we danced to some Beatles song. Neither one of us wanted to be there. No, if a boy were interested in me, it would be because it was his choice to ask me out, not someone else's.

Whenever Dave's fieldwork brought him back to the home office, our eyes would meet as we passed one another on the way to the break room for morning coffee. I kind of wanted to get to know him. Maybe, I thought, I won't become the dreaded spinster I've read about in my favorite books. Every day, I'd promise myself that if I saw him, I'd say, "Hi, I like your tie," or "The weather sure is nice, isn't it?" And every time, my tongue would stay glued to the roof of my mouth.

Dave was the one who broke our staring contest. For once, we were alone in the small, messy break room. "Coffee?" he asked, handing me a hot Styrofoam cup.

"Thanks," I said. I wanted cream, but his body was too close to the container. I decided to skip the cream.

He poured his own, and after a few sips and tentative looks, he said, "Um, I wonder if you'd like to go to dinner and then catch a movie with me on Friday?"

My eyes widened. A boy wanted to take me out on a date. Now what do I say? I tried to look confident as I sipped my coffee. It tasted bitter, and I wished I'd reached for that cream. I was torn and wanted to say, "Sorry, I don't date coworkers." But he was

friendly and handsome, and it was time to leave my parents'
home.

"We could double with Martha if you'd feel more
comfortable."

"Sure," I managed to say as the be-polite rule kicked in. "That
sounds like fun."

"Good. Martha says she knows where you live. We'll pick you
up at six. We can have dinner, then see *2001: A Space Odyssey*. It's
gotten great reviews."

I had nothing else to add to this awkward conversation. Our
date was confirmed. I thought, If Martha is behind this, I'm going
to kill her.

"I need to get back," I said, giving him a fake smile. "See you
Friday."

By the time I reached my department, I was light-headed from
holding my breath. This was a leftover practice from childhood.
Breath-holding numbed my emotions and was now second nature.
I looked up. Martha gave me a high five.

At lunch, she said, "Before you accuse me of setting you up, I
didn't. He's interested in you. He told me you came across as a bit
timid and asked if we should double if you said yes. You can do
this!"

At dinner that night, I told my mom I had a date. "His name
is David. I think you'll like him."

Mom never questioned my infrequent dating or lack of
friends. I never understood her silence. Over the years, my
coworkers told stories about how their parents set their dating age
and curfew. Often, they would laugh and describe how their
moms gave them the facts-of-life speech. Some were funny, yet I
had no desire to share my story. My facts of life were presented to
me in a paperback book around age 12. In sizeable, bold, blood-
red print, the title read *The Facts of Life and Love for Teenagers*. "If
you have any questions, let me know," Mom said as she left my
bedroom.

Her inability to look me in the eye and her quick departure

made me confident I would never ask questions. Yet the pages were yellow and well-worn by the end of my teen years. Repeatedly, I read the chapter, *So, You Want to Have Sex?* And with every read, I decided no, I don't.

The week flew by. Dave was out of the building more than he was at his desk, which helped stop some of my obsessing about everything that could go wrong with our date. Still, my stomach felt queasy when I got home from work that Friday.

The queasy feeling worsened when I entered my bedroom and saw my favorite lavender wool sweater and black slacks on my bed. I stood for a long moment and willed myself not to scream, "Dammit, why tonight, Mom? I finally have a date, and I'm still treated like a child. You've laid out what you wanted me to wear my entire life. Now it's time to stop."

Yet had I ever told her to stop? No, the good girl I had to be was always present, just as she was now. I would make no waves.

"You look very pretty," she said when I appeared in the front room. I gave her an annoyed look, still miffed over her desire to control me.

"I hope you have a good time," she continued. Me too, I thought.

The doorbell rang at precisely 6 p.m. A handsome young man dressed in casual slacks and a cabled V-neck sweater stood before me. His grin was contagious. I smiled, too.

"Come in and meet my parents," I said.

Both sat on the couch and looked like model parents with happy faces, proud to meet their daughter's date. I introduced them. Dad stood, wavered, and then extended a hand. A near-empty glass and bottle of Falstaff beer sat on the end table. His weekend binge was well underway. After a few minutes of idle chitchat, we said our goodbyes and left.

I slowly exhaled as Dave opened the passenger door to his dark blue Chevy Impala. Glancing in the back seat, I saw Martha and her boyfriend connected like two puzzle pieces. Dave was cute, but I couldn't imagine getting that close to anyone.

"Hope everyone is hungry," Dave said. "Next stop, Ruby's Family Restaurant." The evening passed. I said little and was eager to get back home.

I wasn't sure if there would be a second date or even if I wanted one. Dave didn't seem to think I was too weird, and when he asked me for a second date, I heard my parents' voices telling me it was time for me to get married and not to let this one go. The good girl said, "yes."

Over the next four months, we went out for ice cream, took long walks in the woods, and tried our hand at miniature golf. With each date, I relaxed more. We talked about where we went to high school, world events, and our jobs. One night, after we saw *Funny Girl*, we had dinner and talked about our parents.

"Mine are pretty overprotective," I said. "My mom has a lot of mental problems, and my dad likes to drink. A lot. He worries about my mom, but I guess he must. She's not very stable."

"I'm sorry about that," Dave replied, with just the right amount of concern and caring.

He understands, I thought. Now, that's a plus.

"My folks are great," he said. "Have you ever been to Wisconsin?"

"I went to the Dells when I was younger."

"My folks have a small summer home in New Lisbon. It's called 'The Land of OZ.'"

"OZ?" I repeated with a quizzical look.

"Yes, my dad's name is Otto, and my mom's is Zita. So, OZ it is."

That amused me to no end.

"Like that, huh?" he laughed. "We'll go up there sometime if you want."

"I would like that," I said.

When his serious kisses started, I wasn't thrilled and didn't want more. I felt no passion or desire to commit to this man who seemed to like me. Maybe, I thought, I'm just a late bloomer.

Dave and I never got the chance to visit OZ. The year was

1969, and his birth month and year were tied to the draft lottery. When his number was called, he had only two weeks before he reported for boot camp, so we didn't have much alone time. On our last night together, Dave wanted a quiet evening. We decided on takeout pizza that we ate on my parents' patio. I remember prolonged periods of silence. We both started sentences, looked at each other, and then stopped.

My mother broke our silence. "Have you two gone to sleep out here?"

Dave laughed, then grinned. "No, ma'am, we're awake," he said, pulling his lawn chair closer to mine. He took my hands in his. "Look, I'm not good at good-byes, and I have an early morning flight, so I guess I need to leave. Are you gonna miss me?"

He continued before I responded. "Because I'm gonna miss you. I know we've not dated long, but I like you, Linda. Lots! You caught my eye the first day I saw you. I wish world events were different, but I must do my duty."

I avoided direct eye contact. It was easier to talk to the top of his head. "I know you gotta go, and I'm very proud of you." And I was. He was serving our country, which was important to me. Yet I was mad at fate. Not fair, I wanted to shout. I finally meet someone who likes me, and before I can figure out why I don't like him back the same way, he's being taken from me. Just plain no fair!

"Will you wait for me and write often? I know that's a lot to ask."

"Sure," I said. "I'll wait."

My feelings shifted again. Part of me still wanted a way out of this relationship, so I asked, "But won't you be too busy to write?"

"Don't worry, I'll always find time for you," he said, rising from his lawn chair. "Now," he said as he pulled me into his arms, "give me a kiss. I'll be back home before you know it."

Then, poof, he was gone, and I felt the terrified feeling exit my body.

After his eight weeks of boot camp, Dave came home on a week's leave. The phone rang late on a Saturday afternoon. Mom picked it up and then yelled, "It's your boyfriend."

"Hi, sweetheart, I'm home. I missed you," he said. "My mom wants you to come over for Sunday dinner tomorrow. I'll be back at Fort Polk by Thanksgiving, so she wants a big turkey dinner. I'll pick you up around 10, and then we can have some time alone before we head back to my folks' house."

"Can't wait," I said, wondering where my joy was.

The November air was crisp, with a hint of snow. I wore wool slacks and a turtleneck sweater that met my mother's approval.

"It's wonderful to see you again," he said, kissing me quickly. "Let's drive to our favorite spot along the river and catch up."

Even though Dave had the car heater on high, I shivered as we drove along. He looked so different. His carefully combed hair was now an army buzz cut. His brown eyes appeared larger, his nose more prominent. He felt like a man now, but I still felt like an unsure young woman who didn't know who she was. Or what she wanted.

He parked the car in a secluded spot meant for lovers. "Here, let me warm you up," he said as he took me in his arms. His kisses were passionate, and I tried hard to return them. But the internal fireworks were not there.

"Before we head back to my house, I need to tell you that I applied to Officer Training School. I know I will be sent overseas and gone for over two years. I hope you'll wait?"

I didn't answer.

Dave and I saw each other as much as his mother and other friends would allow that week. Our last night together was dinner at a fancy Italian restaurant in the city. The low lights, candles, and soft music added to the atmosphere and my uneasiness. Coy hints and looks had passed around his family while we had been together for the pre-Thanksgiving dinner. I felt a proposal would happen before the night was over.

After our orders were taken, two glasses of red wine were set down before us. I preferred white wine. Red wine reminded me of communion wine, which reminded me that I had to be a good girl. Our conversation felt strained, and I was glad when the main meal arrived. There were prolonged periods of silence as Dave looked numerous times over his shoulder. I almost asked what was so interesting, but I knew what his plan was the instant I became aware of the violinist who strolled from table to table.

My heart raced, and my stomach clenched. I needed time and whispered, "I must visit the little girls' room. I'll be right back."

I was alone and looked in the mirror and saw a young, pretty woman with green eyes. She looked like she was about to be executed. I hurt for her—for the me who had not yet tasted life and what it had to offer.

My first thought was maybe if I stay in the bathroom long enough, the guy with the violin will pass by our table. The second thought was, Get ahold of yourself. You've sensed this coming for weeks. You've even practiced saying, "Yes, Dave, I will marry you."

You know Dave is kind. He also has a great family who laugh and tell corny jokes. And, most importantly, he's the first person who said he wants you. Do you understand that? He. Wants. You. I know that scares the shit out of you because you believe you don't deserve anything good. But, Linda, you need to take this good thing and make the best of it. You may never have another chance. So, when you return to that table, you will say yes. Understand?

I did understand and, as I took one more look in the mirror, I mouthed yes, then fussed with my hair, pinched my cheeks so it looked like I was alive, and returned to the table and the violinist, who was still roving.

"You OK?"

"Sure," I smiled. "Everything is fine."

Eating was hard, as I heard the violinist moving closer. Soon, he stood before our table. The music became softer, sweeter, and more romantic. Dave handed me a small blue box he pulled from his suit jacket pocket. "I picked it out myself," he said. "I hope you like it."

As I opened the box, he reached over to my cold, clammy hand and said, "Linda, I love you, and I'm asking, will you marry me?"

I closed my wet eyes, held my breath, and heard my rehearsed words run through my mind. Now I needed to say them out loud. It took everything I had, but, slowly, I let out my breath, put a smile on my face, and, through tears, said, "Yes, Dave, I will marry you."

As he slipped the ring on my finger and placed a kiss on my lips, the violinist played a happy tune and moved on.

"We'll set the date when my tour of duty is over," he said as he picked up his glass of wine and finished the last of his spaghetti.

"Sure," I answered. As the diamond sparkled, I pushed my plate away. No more pasta fit in my stomach, as it was filled to the brim with uncertainty. What had I done? Yes, I wanted to escape from under my parents' thumb, but wasn't there another way?

But again, for the hundredth time, I heard my high school counselor say, "You're not college material. Just find some nice guy to support you." Nobody asked if that's what I wanted. Nobody cared. So, I sat with a diamond on my finger that felt more like a noose around my neck.

Dave left the next day and was sent to Vietnam a few months later. We wrote letters and signed them with "love," but my heart could not find mine.

# Chapter 5

## *An Affair and a Reluctant Bride*

Soon after Dave left for Vietnam, I lost my job at the insurance company. Then I started working for twelve men who delivered water to people's homes.

"It's nice to have you here," they all said after I'd been there a few weeks. "Our last girl didn't do nothin' but give orders. At least you smile."

"And you look good, too," one of them said with a wink and a toss of his head.

I wasn't sure what that meant, but I suspected it might not have been an innocent comment. I was 24, I'd discovered Harlequin romances, and even though the scenes weren't explicit, they were enough to make me realize there was more to this sexual stuff than I had imagined.

The front office where I worked was small and cramped. I sat at one end, and Raymond, the men's supervisor and my boss, sat in the opposite corner. A long, cluttered table the men used to fill out paperwork occupied the rest of the space.

I reported for work most mornings amid the chaos of twelve men preparing their deliveries. It was a busy, noisy time, and I was always relieved when the last man left. Once things quieted down, Raymond would stop by my desk to check in. He was about five foot five, with a tiny waist and well-developed muscles from carrying large loads of bottled water. With his curly brown hair and crooked smile, he looked like a little boy who knew how to steal cookies and get away with it.

But Raymond knew how to do much more than steal cookies.

When the guys left in the morning, it was guaranteed they wouldn't be back until late afternoon. As I filed sales receipts, phone orders, and reminders into the men's folders, Raymond's eyes kept following me. No, I thought. I've read too many romances.

I didn't react the first time Raymond's hand brushed across my breasts while he explained a new part of the job to me. Maybe it was just an accident?

One day, while I was at my desk, I sensed his eyes on me. Then I felt his hand slide through the V in my sweater and touch my skin. I inhaled deeply as a shiver ran through me.

"Did you like that?" he asked, as he gave each breast a quick squeeze.

I did, but wasn't I supposed to say no?

He then laughed and asked, "Maybe someday I'll be able to see them?"

I was stunned by what happened. It triggered a wave of longing in me that I had never experienced before. My full breasts, which I disliked and felt embarrassed about, were now noticed in a way I couldn't ignore.

The next day, I debated whether I should wear the dress I'd made to the office. I'd learned to knit when I was 10 and had progressed from simple winter scarves to sweaters and, finally, the dress I was about to squeeze myself into. Why not, I thought. I'm proud of it. The dress was knit on tiny needles and took over eight months to complete. When I finally finished, it was smaller than the pattern indicated and clung to my body like a diver's wetsuit. I wasn't sure how I would bend over if I dropped something, but I decided I would worry about that if it happened.

I couldn't believe the power I felt when I walked into the office in that dress. Heads turned. Eyes flicked over me as if I were someone worth noticing. I thought I had no sex appeal, but I was wrong. I had enough to make half a dozen men stumble over their feet.

After that, as the months went on, Raymond went out less on calls and found more excuses to stay by my desk. Sometimes he'd ask about the weather or if I'd seen a particular TV show or movie, and other days he'd stare at my cleavage before running his hand up my skirt. My ability to flirt with my eyes and body language grew stronger. It was intoxicating. I didn't stop him.

Raymond and I would take inventory every Friday morning in the dark warehouse. While he moved pallets of water with a forklift, I verified the numbers he called out to me. When our numbers matched, we returned to the main office.

The morning my world changed, I wore an angora sweater and a short skirt. Raymond declared "inventory time." It was earlier than usual. I grabbed my clipboard and followed him into the warehouse.

"You're looking mighty sexy today."

"I am?"

"Yes, you are," he said. "Let me take that clipboard."

He stepped toward me, cupped my breasts in his hands, and said, "I bet your fiancé likes to see these."

"See them?"

"Like naked. Your fiancé has seen them, right?"

"Uh, no."

"Why not?"

"It seems complicated," I said. "But I guess it's not really."

"Tell me," he said, stepping away from me.

This invitation to spill felt almost too good to be true. Was this the same guy whose hands traveled up my skirts? There was no one else to tell that I didn't want to marry Dave. That Dave never made any sexual moves on me. He acted more like I was his sister instead of the girl he wanted to marry. I'd never been in a priest's confessional booth, but somehow this dingy, dark warehouse felt like that kind of place. I could confess all that I felt was wrong with me and know someone would listen.

Any fear or "sin" that came to mind burst out in a manic way. My words didn't seem to make any sense. I kept talking until I ran out of thoughts and then stopped mid-sentence. "I'm done," I said, holding out my hands.

"That's a lot of stuff," he said, while again staring at my breasts. "I don't know how to help you with Dave or your family, but if you want, I can show you how amazing sex can feel."

The following Friday, Raymond stopped pretending to count pallets of water. "My offer is still open," he said with a wink. "Are you ready?"

Emotionally scared but physically ready, I followed him out to the warehouse. "Would you like to experience your first orgasm today?"

My eyes grew large. Not knowing what that meant, I whispered, "I guess."

"If you can relax, I can make it happen. Do you trust me?"

At this point, trust was not an issue. My body was in charge, and "no" was not available.

Raymond was strong. I caught a quick glimpse of his gold wedding ring as his left arm wrapped around my waist, and the fingers on his right hand slipped under my short skirt. He pulled down my panties.

I stepped out of them and drew in a breath as his fingers touched places I'd only read about in books.

"Jesus," I managed to say when I could breathe again. "What the hell was that?"

"An orgasm, my lovely lady. And if you want, there can be more where that came from."

"I can only hope so."

That day, my dance with sexuality ignited fiercely. I couldn't get enough of Raymond's fingers. When he suggested we could do more on weekends in his big red truck, I couldn't wait.

I lost my virginity in that truck. There was no orgasm, just a stabbing pain, blood, and an "Are you OK?" from Raymond. The chapter *So You Want to Have Sex* popped into my mind. I wasn't as disgusted with sex as my 12-year-old self imagined I'd be, but I still didn't understand why anyone would want to do this every night.

Love remained a mystery. I knew it wasn't what I felt with Raymond. Dave felt like fear, and Raymond fueled my overwhelming need to experience orgasms. It was Christmas and a year of new experiences. Should I break off my engagement with Dave? While I now knew I could have sex, I couldn't picture myself having sex with Dave.

While I was helping dry dishes one night, I said, "Mom, you know, Dave has been gone for over a year now, and I think I need to break off our engagement. I don't have…"

The chipped white dinner plate Mom was holding slipped from her hand and shattered on the floor before I could finish speaking. I watched her eyes widen as spit gathered on her lips.

"See what you made me do," she screamed. "No daughter of mine will break the heart of a man serving in Vietnam. Do you understand me?"

I stood completely still as I saw visions of my four-year-old self crying hysterically. I didn't remember what I'd done or said, but repeatedly I heard the words, "Mommy, I'll be good, I'll be good. I'm sorry, Mommy. I'll be good."

I didn't dare disobey her. I didn't want to be the one to push my mother over the edge. She had scared me when I was little, and she scared me now. I saw so much of myself in her. Eventually, she pulled herself together, and I swallowed my desire to break off my engagement.

I don't remember who cleaned up the broken pieces. I immediately threw my wet dish towel on the floor and ran to my bedroom. I needed someone to hold me, but there was no one around, so I grabbed my pillow and held it to my chest.

Damn it, I didn't want to be married, period. Now what am I supposed to do? I thought. I'm working for a water company that's paying me minimum wage. I have a small savings account, but it won't last long. I have no friends I can vent to. I haven't gone to college or experienced being on my own. No one in this smothering family has gone to college.

I also don't want to date. Boys don't excite me, but I can't talk about that either. Yes, I'm having an affair with Raymond, but I've never wished he would divorce his wife and marry me. God knows I have to keep that a secret because it would be a disaster if Mom ever found out.

And so the soul-searching continued, and when it was all over, and I'd let go of my pillow, I knew I would do what was expected of me and would not end my engagement.

Today, as I look back, I see a young woman sitting in her bedroom on her pink floral bedspread, who didn't know who she was or who she could become. She was caught up in society's norms and desperately afraid of disobeying her parents. Questions were difficult for her to ask, and she usually preferred to leave her life up to fate rather than risk disturbing her already unstable world.

She also harbored deep, disturbing thoughts that maybe she was what people called gay. She was a sheltered, uninformed, and immature 24-year-old who felt uncomfortable with sexuality in general. She only knew that being gay involved being attracted to the same sex. She had a vague idea that being gay was unacceptable and was only talked about in derogatory terms. She didn't understand why, though.

She thought living with a woman meant they were good friends with similar goals but weren't ready to marry. They would split living expenses, cooking, and household chores. She was unaware that this kind of relationship could also include a sexual element.

She knew in eighth grade and high school that she couldn't stop thinking about two of her female teachers. But she didn't understand why. Repeatedly, she told herself that her fixation on these women was just a desire for a caring mother figure in her life. Nothing more than that. Still, her difficulty forming genuine intimacy with men caused her to question her sexual identity for years to come.

Dave's army assignment kept him moving frequently, so his letters from Vietnam were sporadic. Sometimes it was months before I got a letter, so I was surprised when Mom handed me the envelope.

"Darling, it's official," he wrote. "I'm a short-timer. I will be home for good sometime in May."

The familiar spidery tummy drop happened. I wanted to feel more than just dread. I waited and argued with myself every day. I wanted to escape but didn't know how to make that happen.

Dave wanted to surprise me, so he didn't call when he arrived home. Instead, he drove over and rang the bell. As he stood in the doorway, I froze.

Come on, Linda, respond. Here stands your future husband, I thought to myself.

"I'm home," he said, taking me in his arms. "I've missed you so."

I searched my body for happiness, but I could find none. I didn't say I missed you, too.

He was thinner than when he left, his complexion darker from the tropical sun, and still handsome. But that was all. He didn't stay long that night. "My folks want me to stay close to home—to fatten me up, they said. We can talk on the phone. OK?"

That was fine by me. I needed time to get used to him being back in my day-to-day life again.

It didn't take long for Dave to bring up a wedding date. We were in my living room.

Dave took my hand. "Let's get our date set."

"Sure. How about a fall wedding? October would be nice."

"That's too far away," he said, squeezing my hand. "How about August?"

I thought that was too soon, but he insisted. "I want to marry you as soon as possible."

I couldn't understand his urgency, but I gave in. On Saturday, August 14, I would become Mrs. Linda Cooper.

If there was time after one of our sexual encounters, Raymond would ask me about Dave. "Has Dave seen these lovely ladies yet?" he asked while he helped me put my bra back on.

"Shit, no," I said.

"Why not?"

"He's a good man, but no matter how I try, I can't find the love I'm supposed to feel."

"I'd suggest you break off the engagement," he said, as he gave my bottom one more pat. "It won't work if you feel that way."

I knew he was right, so I decided to go directly to Dave instead of my mother this time. Over the next few days, I built up my courage, and when Dave arrived, I took him over to the sofa in our family room.

I squirmed, stuttered, and said, "I'm so sorry, but I can't do this. I don't want to marry you. Here's your ring. I'm sorry." I was sure he could hear my heartbeat. I know I could.

He sat with a stunned look but slowly and calmly said, "No, Linda, I'm not going to take your ring back. We can work this out. I know you're scared right now. Marriage is a big commitment. I'll leave now, and we'll talk soon." He kissed me quickly, left my ring on the table's edge, and walked out the door.

I rushed to my bedroom and waited for what I knew would come next. It didn't take long for both parents to arrive at my bedroom door.

"What the hell just happened out there?" my dad asked. "And why is your engagement ring on the table?"

"I gave it back, Daddy. I don't love him."

"You know all about love, do you? I'll tell you this right now. Dave is a decent man who served our country. You're lucky to have him. You're 25 years old and still don't have a decent job. What kind of life do you think you can create for yourself? I only have one more thing to say, and it's this: You will leave this home on August 14, even if you are not married. Now think about that."

Mom stood like a statue. Tears streamed down her face. "Your father's right," she said as she left my room. "Dave's a good guy. You'll be sorry if you don't do this."

I left the ring where it was, but I thought about it. I had no other prospects waiting. I hated dating and didn't have a job with any kind of future. I couldn't get credit in my name. Society told me it wasn't proper for me to live alone, which put me right back where I started. Be a good girl, marry, and hope things will work out.

The next day, a bouquet of red roses arrived with a card that read, "I want to marry you. Plan to put the ring back on your finger Wednesday at 7 p.m. Love, Dave."

I yelped as a thorn pricked my finger. Maybe, I thought, this is a sign that Dave is a prince and has come to save me. Deep down, I knew this wasn't true, but there was nothing else to hold on to.

Wednesday night, Dave said we could build a good life together. He already had a job offer and was ready to buy his own car. I wanted to believe him, so I let him put the ring back on my finger.

We planned a small wedding. Both families agreed to invite only close friends and relatives. I didn't want any dancing, so there was no need for a band. Every day, I took one step at a time, doing what society and family expected. My mom planned a shower for a Sunday in July.

I wanted an escape, and Raymond casually told me he would be at the office the morning of my wedding shower if I wanted to stop by. Yes, I wanted to stop by. I wanted—no, needed—to get lost in the moment, where there was no Dave, no upcoming marriage, no controlling parents. There would only be a feeling that I was desired. And for one moment, alive.

Dave and I got married on a rainy afternoon. Dressed in pure white, I stood at the back of the church where every Sunday I was told I was a sinner headed for hell. Would this same minister recognize I was in hell on earth right now? I looked out the open back door of the church as the rain mixed with my tears, thinking it's still not too late to run. My father appeared, took my arm firmly in his, and said, "It's time."

The ceremony was short. I cried through most of it. I wished someone would stand up and object.

I wasn't in a rush to leave for my wedding night, so I took extra time talking with the reception guests and changing out of my wedding dress. Eventually, it was time to go. Dave had booked a fancy hotel room in downtown Chicago. He checked us in as Mr. and Mrs. Cooper. My anxiety increased, and I could feel tears beginning to well up again.

After confirming the bathroom door was locked, I changed into my white negligee and got into bed. But when I saw the look of anticipation on Dave's face, I curled up in a tight ball and refused to be touched. It would have been easier for me to fly to the moon than to have sex.

He didn't push that night. We left for our honeymoon in Seattle the next day. In the air and with a drink in my hand, I lied and told Dave I'd gotten my period.

"How long does it last?" he asked.

I told him a week, even though it was usually only a few days.

When I returned to work, Raymond greeted me.

"So, did you have amazing sex with Dave?"

"No," I replied, "and I still haven't."

Raymond grinned.

"Don't look at me that way, Raymond," I said in a sassy voice. "We're done, too."

That was also a lie. Lunch was spent in his big red truck, where I did what I should have done with my husband.

Raymond's wife found out about us within two months of my marriage. I was making dinner, waiting for Dave to come home, when the phone rang.

The voice was slow, controlled, and icy.

"This is Jill, Raymond's wife. I know you're screwing my

husband. Raymond has terminated your job, so you won't be coming back to the office, and if I ever see you with him again, I will make your life a living hell. Do you understand?"

My heart pounded, and my stomach heaved as bile climbed in my throat. I managed a strained yes, hung up, and then vomited. That night at dinner, I calmly told Dave I quit my job.

"Quit? That's a surprise."

"I've been thinking about finding a new job for a while, and today there was a big office ruckus, so I got mad and quit."

"Good," he said. "I never did like you working with all those men."

# Chapter 6

## *Settling In*

I saw the white coat first, then heard the knock. I'd hoped it was Dr. Bobbi. It wasn't. It was Dr. Braun. Unexplained fear ran through me.

"Good morning, Linda. How was your night?"

I swallowed, grabbed Baby, scooted toward the wall, took a deep breath, and mumbled, "OK."

"Good," he said, dragging a chair to my bedside. "I've prescribed a low dose of Inderal for now. I'll increase it if I need to."

I wanted to ask what Inderal was for, but my anxiety was making it hard for me to talk.

"During our first office visit, you mentioned seeing a little girl who wasn't there. You interacted with her, and I believe you said her name was Noel. Can you tell me more?"

I needed to respond. The quicker I spoke, the sooner I'd get my diagnosis. I held Baby close. "Like what?"

"Does this child do things you aren't aware of?"

"I don't think so."

"Do you ever lose time?"

"What's that mean?"

"It's called dissociation. Some patients lose significant

memories of specific times, people, and events. Others feel as if they're watching a movie of themselves. Did you feel like you watched yourself when you saw Noel?"

"No. We were just … both there in the same room."

I could tell that wasn't the correct answer from his frown. My armpits grew wet.

"With dissociation, someone may experience depression, anxiety, thoughts of suicide, as well as feeling detached from emotions and lacking self-identity," he continued. "Do you have thoughts of suicide?"

I immediately pictured myself in my closed garage with the engine running. I would sit there until my heart was pounding and I thought, *I'm going to pass out.* In a panic, I'd reach for the car keys and turn off the ignition. I didn't want to die. I just wanted to escape the life I was living.

I wasn't ready to admit those thoughts, so I looked up at the ceiling and quietly said, "No." I could tell he didn't believe me by the expression on his face.

"We've just begun the evaluation process and have many more tests to do. Dr. Sachs will be in later. Have a good day," he said, and left my room with his coattails flying.

A few minutes later, dressed in bright colors, Dr. Bobbi arrived in my room like Mary Poppins. The atmosphere seemed to shift, and my spirits immediately lifted. I half expected to hear "spit-spot," but instead, she sat on my bed and said, "Let's see if we can get to know one another better."

I caught a whiff of her perfume, laid Baby on the pillow, and felt my body inch closer to hers. She didn't move away. Whatever I felt for this woman sitting beside me on my bed was still there and, in the light of the new day, had once again flared.

"I'm married and have a son and daughter. And a hundred years ago,"—she raised her eyebrows—"I was a gym teacher. Now I run a private practice and work as an assistant professor at Rush.

"I'm waiting for my accreditation to become a licensed clinical psychologist. Until then, I can't chart. This means the nurse assigned to you will enter the information I give them about our sessions."

I found out many years later that wasn't true—just like so many other things I was told back then.

"What else goes in my chart?"

"The results of your tests and how you handle things while on the ward. Staff will note if you go to activities or stay in your room. You will be assessed for depression or suicidal ideation, what medications you are on and when, and if you have any side effects. It keeps your entire care team informed. But that's not your concern," she said while tucking a piece of hair behind my ear. It was a simple gesture, but it helped strengthen our bond.

I lowered my eyes. "Can my husband see what's in my records?"

"Not unless you give him signed permission."

"I don't want to do that."

"That's your call. Now, I have a question for you," she said, taking my hand.

I reached for Baby. "What kind of question?"

"Have you ever been hypnotized?"

"No." I'd seen hypnotism on a television show once, and it seemed hokey.

"Would you like to try?"

"Umm, why?"

"Because both Buddy and I know that hypnotism can be helpful to get answers from hidden places."

"Who's Buddy?"

"Oh, that's what staff and colleagues call Dr. Braun. You know, I'm Bobbi, and he's Buddy."

Those nicknames didn't sound right. I was used to calling everyone Mr. or Mrs. or Doctor.

"Anyway," Dr. Bobbi went on, "hypnotism doesn't hurt, and this session will only last a few minutes. I will count backward from ten to one. Are you ready?"

She placed her index finger on the middle of my forehead. "Close your eyes and go inside."

Her counting was slow and rhythmic. She instructed me to relax and go deeper with each descending number. When she reached one, she quietly said, "Now I want you to tell me if your body feels heavy and relaxed?"

I was unsure but wanted to please, so I said, "Um, yes."

"Good. Is your name Judy?"

I giggled. "No."

"Is your name Linda?"

"Yes."

"And are you at Rush right now?"

"Uh-huh."

"Are you married?"

"Yes."

"Good, you're doing fine. Tell me, Linda, how old do you feel right now?"

I didn't know why Dr. Bobbi was asking this question, so I blurted out the first age that came to mind. "Four, maybe?"

"Do you have a name?"

"No," I thought. Didn't I tell you yesterday I didn't like names? And with that, I opened my eyes and stuck my thumb in my mouth.

"That was highly successful," she said with a smile and a quick squeeze of my hand. "You will be an excellent candidate for hypnosis. Expect more as time goes on."

When she left, I pulled out my journal and pen and wrote:

*September 6, 1985*

*Dr. Bobbi said she hypnotized me today and I did good. But I think she's wrong. I didn't feel any different than I do now. I wasn't relaxed like she said I should be. And I didn't go deep, whatever that means. But I guess if hypnosis brings this pretty lady to my room, I'll do whatever she asks.*

Early in the afternoon, Vicki came into my room with a packet of questions about my moods. She explained it was a depression survey required for all new patients. It was supposed to be a short test, but because I never knew how I felt, the questions seemed to go on forever. Even as a child, feelings never made sense.

Vicki observed my clenched fingers and stiff body as we reached the end. "You did good. I'll get us a snack, and then we can continue."

The snack was peanut butter crackers from a vending machine. I ate them slowly because I wanted to delay the next item on Vicki's list: my family history.

I shared the basics. "My mom was born in Germany, and my dad's family came from Yugoslavia." I then discussed my mom's mental health issues and my father's family history of alcoholism.

"Do you have brothers or sisters?"

"No sisters. Just two younger brothers. We're not close," I answered. Some siblings form bonds to deal with family issues. We were a family who did not.

These were my core truths. Anything extracted from me in future therapy sessions would all be fabricated fantasy.

"That's all I know," I said. "Can we stop now?"

"I know this is hard for you. We're almost finished," Vicki said. "One more question. Dr. Braun indicated one reason you're here is because your marriage has fallen apart."

"Yes, it has."

"In what way?"

"I don't love him."

"Is that all?"

Damn it! No, that's not all, I thought as I held my breath and let tears form. I can't do this. All those words like "masturbate," "orgasm," "breast," "vagina," "penis" are stuck deep inside and won't come out. You can't—my mind shrieked—tell anyone what you've done.

"Linda, what's going on? Who's here?" Vicki gently asked.

Startled, I jumped. "Nobody's here. I just can't talk about sex and what I do." I grabbed Baby, stuck my thumb in my mouth, and refused to say another word.

Dr. Braun didn't come back that week, but Dr. Bobbi

appeared between other patient sessions. She didn't talk about hypnosis or ask how I was feeling. Instead, she would just ruffle my hair, say hi to Baby, or put her finger inside her cheek. I giggled at the pop every time.

When she would leave, I'd replay what she did or said. I'd feel her hands run through my hair and see her smile. I'd smile, too, and then wait—hour after hour—for her to return. I was overwhelmed with emotions, their definitions as elusive as the dust motes I'd seen in Dr. Braun's office.

My new roommate, Harriet, arrived late Saturday afternoon with a suitcase the size of a carpetbag. She was tall and thin, with a pixie haircut that made her eyes look like two blue marbles. When she stared at Baby and me, I quickly looked away. She reeked of cigarettes. On her feet were silver-colored tennis shoes, which fascinated me.

The nurse asked me to leave the room while she got Harriet settled in. I wanted to say no, but I decided maybe it was time to explore. I'd been on the ward for four days and had not left my room. I held Baby in my left arm, stuck my right thumb in my mouth, and exited the room, terrified of what I might see.

There were pictures on the wall I had missed the night Vicki showed me around. Images of oceans, trees, and meadows were interspersed with still-life paintings. They briefly brought me back to my high school art classes and my favorite teacher, Mrs. Anderson In my yearbook, she had wished me a bright and happy life.

I guess that didn't happen, I thought. As I headed toward the windowless common room, I was struck by the starkness of the ward. Aside from the pictures, there were no warm colors, eye-catching vases with flowers, or what my mother-in-law called "pretty-pretties." Instead, I could only detect bleach mixed with the overwhelming smell of bodies exuding fear and despair.

The door labeled "O.T." was open. I looked inside and saw a small group of patients focused on drawing with crayons and markers.

A pretty woman with a jet-black braid down her back said, "Welcome. You're Linda, right? I was planning to stop by today and arrange a time to meet, but you can join us now if you'd like."

I shook my head no. I didn't have any interest in arts and crafts.

"What the hell she got a doll for?" a middle-aged, grossly overweight lady with long, stringy hair and too much makeup asked. "She ain't no kid."

"That's not appropriate, Donna," the woman said.

"Yeah, Donna," a young man who wore a food-stained shirt and displayed an arm with numerous deep cuts said. "Maybe she's crazy like you." And then he laughed and laughed.

"That's enough," the woman said to the group, and then turned back to me. "Sorry. Now, about that—can I see you later? Here are some crayons, markers, and paper. You can draw in your room until then."

I took my thumb out of my mouth, accepted the items, and left the room. I passed two more patients who, like me, had no laces in their shoes. I picked up my pace and headed back to my room. The only signs of Harriet were a bunch of wadded-up clothes on the bed, an open pack of cigarettes on her tray table, and her worn blue toothbrush by the sink.

Harriet was a hall walker and smoked whenever she had the chance. When she wasn't smoking, she watched TV. I was thrilled. She was never in the room. I loved being alone.

# Chapter 7

## *She Won't Be Back*

It was the middle of week two. Harriet had been discharged a day earlier, so I was alone again. It was time to venture out to the dining room. I had promised Dr. Bobbi I would try to eat with the other patients. I'd gone for short hallway walks with Baby and had managed to ask for my curling iron, but I didn't dare eat with everyone.

Standing in the doorway, I spotted the overweight lady and the guy with the same food-stained shirt. I exhaled slowly and chose a seat as far away from them as possible. I sat Baby in the next chair and got my food. I didn't interact with patients or staff. I learned that people would forget I was there if I didn't answer. I'd become invisible and be left alone.

Everyone ate what was on their menu or went hungry. There were usually the same two options on the weekly menu we all had to fill out. All meals were served on dull gray, unbreakable plates or bowls on a metal tray. When meals were finished, you carried your tray to a designated spot. A staff member would check to ensure the required plastic fork and all-purpose spoon were still there. Only then were you allowed to leave.

That night, the dining area felt peaceful. All I heard were chairs being pulled closer to tables, snippets of conversations mixed with swear words, and the sounds of kitchen staff scraping food off plates into trash cans. I kept my eyes on my plate, which held an overly breaded chicken breast, instant mashed potatoes with salty gravy, and something that looked like peas. Tears welled up, and I wondered why I had agreed to be admitted to a psychiatric ward. I'd seen little of Dr. Braun and hoped his promise of a diagnosis and treatment plan would be worth all the anxiety I was feeling. I didn't want to spend another minute in the dining room. So, I stood, ate the last of my soggy cherry pie, picked up Baby from her chair, and left as unnoticed as when I arrived.

Back in my room, I sat Baby on my bed pillow and pulled over the tray table. I took out my journal and started writing about how I kept my promise to Dr. Bobbi when a lady in a white coat knocked on my door. "Good evening. I'm Dr. King. Did you have a nice dinner?"

I gave her a blank stare. I didn't remember anyone telling me another doctor would be coming to see me.

"Dr. Braun asked me to stop in and see you," she said as she pushed the table out of the way. "Your chart notes say you dissociated when your nurse asked questions about your marriage. And from some of your behaviors, your team has begun to suspect you may have deep-seated sexual issues. I work with many abused patients, so Dr. Braun thought I could dig a little deeper for a cause."

My fear detector went off. Right away, I didn't trust her. She seemed too bossy, and her sweet perfume made me think of funeral flowers.

Abused? My mind whirled. When had I said I'd been abused?

"What kind of questions?" I asked as I reached for Baby.

"She won't be needed." Dr. King took Baby from me and dropped her on the floor. "Now I want you to lie on the bed."

I didn't want to lie down. I wanted Baby. I tried to defy her, but her eyes and face looked like Mommy's when she meant business.

"So," she said as she inched closer to me, "did any friend or relative ever give you a kiss that didn't feel right?"

"No, but…" I lifted my arms and tried to sit up. "I want Baby."

"You can have her when we're done," she said, pushing my arms back down and holding them. I was pinned. I could feel the sticky pie I'd gulped down earlier moving into my throat.

"Did anyone in the family, like an uncle, ask you to play a special secret game with them?"

My eyes grew large with fear. I knew what that meant. "No!" I shouted.

"Your chart says there is alcoholism on your father's side. Did your father drink at home?"

I squeaked out a yes.

"Did he ever come into your bedroom when he was drunk?"

I shook my head violently from side to side.

"What did he do to you?"

"Nothing," I said. I tried to break her hold, but she was much stronger than me.

"Are you sure?" she said as her face moved closer to mine. "What did he do to you?"

"Nothing, nothing—let me go!"

"Is this the reason you can't talk about sex?" she asked as she released my arms and placed her hand above my breast. "Did your father touch you here?"

"NO, NO, NO!" I screamed. As her hand brushed across my breast, my body erupted in terror. I couldn't breathe. I couldn't move. Paralyzed, I went silent, watching my body from above and hoping I'd never come back.

I had no clue how long I was stuck in the in-between land. But when I got back to my body, I felt relieved to be in Dr. Bobbi's arms—with Baby and me.

"Hey, cutie, you're back," she said, as she stroked my face and hair. I briefly flinched as a wave of nausea and fear washed over me.

"Shh, shh. I'm right here, and she's gone. You're safe with me right now. God, I'm so sorry," Dr. Bobbi said. "Vicki just went to get you some medication to help calm you down."

I placed my thumb in my mouth and let Dr. Bobbi rock me until I heard Vicki softly say, "The staff is processing what happened. Dr. King will not be allowed to return to this ward. None of what happened here tonight is appropriate therapy. I want you to take this pill, and then I'll help you and Baby get ready for bed. Dr. Bobbi and I will stay with you until you fall asleep."

The next morning, my vision blurred as I woke up to the sound of breakfast. For a moment, I wondered where I was. Then a flood of memories returned, and panic took over. Where was Baby? I sat up. The room spun briefly before calming down. I saw Baby in pajamas. Vicki or Dr. Bobbi had placed her within reach. I picked her up, wondered what I'd been given to make me feel so spaced out, pulled the bedcovers over us, and drifted back into nothingness.

When I woke again, Dr. Bobbi was standing next to my bed.

"Hey, sweetie," she said with the smile I was growing to love. "I think it's time for you to start your day. Buddy and I just met with your team. With the weekend coming up and the terrible experience last night, we decided to skip therapy until Monday. I'll stop by often, like I always do."

I smiled back at her, but the ability to talk was still stuck deep within.

During one of her many visits, Dr. Bobbi told me I needed to be easily observed, so I had to keep my door wide open. Over the next four days, staff watched a catatonic woman who pretended to feed Baby the meals delivered to her room. I scribbled on paper with crayons from my art supplies. I sucked my thumb, stared into space, answered all questions with head shakes, and read *The World of Pooh* from cover to cover.

# Chapter 8

## *Sand Trays*

"Good morning," Dr. Bobbi said early Monday. "I've read your chart notes and see you still refuse to speak, so I want you to try something today. It's just down the hall. You won't have to talk, and you can take Baby with you. Can you come with me, please?"

Slowly, I nodded yes, picked up Baby, and followed Dr. Bobbi down a long side corridor near the locked metal door that led to the outside world. I cast a longing look at it as I passed by.

"It's right in here," Dr. Bobbi said, stopping at a closed door. The brass nameplate had an unpronounceable doctor's name on it. I backed up and shook my head no.

"It's OK, Linda. We're not here to see this doctor," she said, opening the door. "What I want you to do is in this room."

An older woman with green-rimmed glasses and red hair sat behind a small, dark gray desk. "This wonderful lady is this doctor's secretary and the keeper of these toys," Dr. Bobbi said, squeezing my hand.

Toys? I thought. What toys?

I turned my head and took in the most incredible sight. Along the far wall were three six-foot-long wooden shelves, each holding items that looked like they came from numerous dollhouses. There were miniature people, animals, furniture, religious artifacts—more than my overwhelmed mind could process. Below was a wooden box on a metal stand with wheels. The box's sky-blue interior contained three to four inches of smooth white sand.

"This is called a sand tray," Dr. Bobbi said. "It's used to help people who have experienced trauma or abuse."

Damn, I thought, there's that word again. *Abuse?* I held my breath as Dr. Bobbi continued.

"All I want you to do today is choose whatever toys catch your eye and create a picture of your world. There's no right or wrong way to build. I'll leave and come back when you're finished. Do you think you can do that?"

I nodded yes, tucked Baby into my left arm, and scanned the shelves. This looked like it could be fun. So many toys—where should I start? I let the sand run through my fingers. I hesitated briefly, wondering how to fit my messy world into an 18-by-20-inch rectangular box. That seemed impossible, so I decided to build a small model of the neighborhood I grew up in.

I found plastic figures in the people category to represent me, my mom, dad, and two brothers. It was hard to position the figures as I wanted while holding Baby, so I set her at the foot of the tray where I could still see her.

A black-and-white dog caught my attention. Penny came to mind. I quickly kissed the figure and placed it beside me to represent all the dogs in my life. My immediate family, with plastic smiles, stood before me, and I felt pleased. Next, I found a few houses, a red schoolhouse with a bell, and set a small stack of multicolored books in front of one of the houses. I then lined the imaginary street with a replica of our family car and numerous trees. Carefully, I placed yellow eyes in the branches and, with my fingers, drew long lines in the sand for the roads.

This first tray was based on reality. It felt creative and freeing. There were no rules I had to follow, and best of all, no one was there to tell me I did something wrong. My second tray was the zoo. In those early trays, I built only what I knew.

But as Dr. Braun started to ask what I later realized were carefully planned questions, it wasn't long before items like coffins, crosses, and blood-red stones appeared in my trays. I wasn't yet aware that Dr. Braun had decided I had been part of a cult. The power of his suggestions—along with the drugs and his firm belief that I'd been in a cult—were too strong to resist. Looking back, I see that it was then that I fell into a trap with no way out.

What Dr. Bobbi didn't tell me that day was the tray I built in belonged to a Jungian analyst. When his patients used the sand tray, he viewed the items and scenes as symbols of their insecurities, fears, phobias, and dreams. I learned years later that Dr. Bobbi had never been trained in using sand trays. She didn't follow the prescribed Jungian protocols. Instead, she interpreted what I placed in my tray as actual events I had experienced.

All my main sessions with Dr. Bobbi took place in the sand tray room and were discussed again hours later in my room on my bed. Sand trays became my "therapy" sessions. I was never taken to a conference room or office for traditional talk therapy. Instead, when Dr. Bobbi came to my room, I put a handmade sign on my door that read *"In session. Do not enter."*

By the end of my hospitalization, our doctor-patient relationship became even more blurred. Every morning, she'd drop her huge Gucci purse behind my bed, claiming she trusted me and had nowhere else to keep it. On many late afternoons, she would stick that same *"In Session"* sign on my door, make her way to my bed, then lay her head on my lap and take a nap.

Dr. Braun usually pulled up the guest chair or stood, his bulky frame towering over me as he asked if I knew certain facts about cults. He would increase my medication dose if I appeared confused or refused to answer, so it was clear I had to come up with whatever lie popped into my head as quickly as possible.

I realize now that in my four years at Rush, I never had a single legitimate therapy session that met recognized professional standards. Even though, at that time, I wasn't mentally capable of understanding what was happening to me, I was never given a chance to sit across from a therapist and discuss my home life, marriage, or uncontrollable compulsions.

By the time I arrived on the ward, Dr. Braun had thoroughly indoctrinated all his hand-picked staff with his belief that satanic cults were rapidly gaining ground. Everyone on the ward was considered a cult victim, even if we denied what we confessed under hypnosis, direct questioning, or, in my case, in sand trays.

The staff was well-versed in cult symbols, holidays, and supposed ceremonies. So, while I had imagined eyes in the trees to symbolize my lifelong feeling of being watched—as a child and now by the staff—Dr. Bobbi interpreted those same eyes as proof that I was signaling cult surveillance, warning that if I revealed what I knew, there would be consequences.

These trays I so readily built would become my jailers. For me, they served two purposes: first, they gave me something to do besides stare at my four walls; and second, they satisfied my compulsive need to repeat the same action. These bullshit trays became my new obsession—one I got rewarded for.

# Chapter 9

## *Finger Signals*

It was late afternoon. I had waited silently all day for Dr. Bobbi to come back to my room. When she blew in with her magic smile, all my frustration disappeared.

"Ready to go back to the sand room?"

I nodded yes.

"If I told you I could help you talk without using your words, would you be interested?"

I wrinkled my nose while my head bobbed like a famous bobblehead.

"Good," she said. "This technique is called ideo-motor signals, or responses. I call them finger signals. All you need to do is give me your hand, and I'll teach you how to let your fingers answer my questions."

I wasn't sure what that meant, but I was all in if I didn't have to answer questions verbally.

This was a simple process. I trusted Dr. Bobbi and placed my open dominant hand on her palm. Her voice was calm, almost meditative, as she carefully explained that my index finger would be my "yes" finger, my middle finger would be my "no," and my thumb would be my "stop." That was all—yes, no, stop.

Dr. Bobbi could then ask me open-ended questions—those

that could be answered with just a yes, no, or stop. Easy, straightforward? Yes, it was. But this technique, like the sand tray, was misused.

In the 1800s, when this technique was developed, it was believed that finger signals allowed more accurate information to come from the unconscious mind through ideo-motor responses rather than verbal responses. However, the practice was discredited over time. In the 1980s, when I was hospitalized, finger signals were not considered a reputable psychological treatment tool. Dr. Bobbi used them anyway.

My mind and fingers were trained like a monkey in a lab to give the "correct" response. I quickly learned that when I verbally gave Dr. Bobbi a "no" answer—as in, "No, nobody in my family took me to a meeting where people wore black robes"—all she had to do was sigh, frown, and then ask for my hand. I could feel her displeasure in my "no" answer as profoundly as if I'd been slapped.

Once she had my hand, she'd ask me the same question again. This time, when my "yes" finger rose, I was rewarded with praise. "Good," she'd say, seeming to take pleasure from the perverse scenes that were eventually depicted in the sand.

"You understand, Linda, that even though you said no, there's a part inside you that knows you were taken somewhere. Now that part is finally able to reveal the truth. More parts will confess over time. So, can you tell me how old you were when you first saw people in black robes?"

At first, this felt crazy making. Who believes a raised finger over a human verbal response? But, like everything else, the more I allowed my "yes" finger to rise, the easier it became. I simply let my finger say "yes." It felt like a game I had to play to earn the praise I compulsively sought.

Because if I didn't play the game the way I'd been taught— with the rules I'd been programmed with—I'd be accused of not wanting to improve. Or when she grew frustrated with me, she'd quietly say, "Fingers don't lie, Linda." In other words, I was lying if I said no to anything. Always, I was told some unknown part inside knew better than I did.

"So," Dr. Bobbi asked, "did you like making this tray?"

My "yes" finger rose.

"Do you want to make another one?"

The same finger rose.

"Is that you and your family over there?"

My "yes" finger rose again.

"I see a house and books. Do you like scary books?"

My "no" finger rose.

"Did you like school?"

My "no" finger rose. That surprised me because I thought I liked school.

"Are those lines in the sand rivers?"

Again, my "no" finger rose straight and tall.

"What are they?"

This wasn't a yes-or-no question. It was a question that needed an answer. What was I going to do? My lines weren't rivers, and I had to tell her. For the first time in four days, in a child's voice, I said, "Dey is woads."

She squeezed my hand firmly. "That's enough for today. You did well. Now, remember, other patients share this tray, so it's important to return all the items to their original spots. Only Buddy or me should see your tray. I'll see you later."

I don't recall Dr. Braun ever being in the sand room when Dr. Bobbi asked me about the contents of my trays. This allowed her to ask leading questions and interpret what she saw and what I said. Since she couldn't chart and had to relay everything to the nurse on duty, I often wondered how much misinformation was recorded in my records.

That day, though, I believed my fingers were magic. Maybe, I thought, these sand trays and finger signals could unlock everything. In my mind's eye, I could picture Dr. Bobbi asking me questions about my sexual desires. I then saw my truthful fingers answering the questions from my unconscious. It would be so easy, because I wouldn't have to use the words that still wouldn't come out of my mouth. The truth would be revealed and unlocked from its hidden place and, at long last, I'd know why I did what I did.

I then imagined myself going home. I'd be free of obsessive thoughts. Dave and I would have deep conversations and gradually build a real marriage, maybe even have a baby. Sure, I'd have work to do. I'd return to therapy. But hallelujah, I'd understand what was wrong with me. I'd finally get my diagnosis and treatment plan and start heading toward a happy life.

How much I wished that scenario could be true. But it wasn't. Time would prove that Dr. Bobbi and her unorthodox therapies were no different than my compulsive need for orgasms. I needed her love and acceptance. She was all I had to cling to. I convinced myself that she truly cared, wanted to help me, and didn't see the harm being done. This, along with the drugs in my little white pill cup, deepened the cult-like beliefs I was being fed, blurring the line between reality and fantasy forever.

While I dismantled the tray that day, I wondered where the child's voice had come from. My whole body felt incredibly young —maybe three? I had imagined myself being young when I drank from my baby bottle or used a pacifier, but I knew I was an adult. Even sucking my thumb didn't come from where I had just spoken. No, that voice felt different from anything I had experienced.

Looking back, I think acting, feeling, and talking like a child was probably the only way I knew how to deal with everything. Everything—from the medications I was given to being locked up —was more than my already anxious mind could handle. Naturally, the scared, overwhelmed part of me retreated deeper inside, where I mostly managed to shield myself from feeling the unfair things happening. The medications dulled my mind and helped numb my emotional pain.

It was clear that my adult self was crumbling. As my sand sessions grew more menacing, I was eager to filter everything through my younger self, who seemed to handle it much better than I did. I, the adult, would be there for the emotionally exhausting, incredibly difficult information I was asked to believe —but then I'd quickly step back, allowing the child to take over.

Making my first tray and experiencing finger signals left me hopeful that I had a new communication method. But again, I was wrong.

# Chapter 10

## *Compulsion Returns*

The next day, Dr. Braun finally came to my room after breakfast and meds. I saw him in the doorway, picked up Baby, and, for the first time, didn't scoot back into the corner. I still felt guarded, but some of my initial fear had eased.

"Good morning, Linda. I see from your chart notes that you experienced a significant setback after the unfortunate incident with Dr. King last week. Are you feeling better today?"

I glared at him but didn't reply. I wanted him to say he was deeply sorry that had happened. Instead, he said, "Dr. King said her approach would be helpful. But it seems she needs more training in working with my patients."

When he didn't say anything else, I wondered again what I had gotten myself into.

"Now, the last time we talked about Noel, you said you named her. But I wonder if you think you have any other parts inside you. Not behavior parts," he went on. "We all have aspects of our personality that present differently—it depends on the day, time, and situations we find ourselves in. I want to know if you have time lapses when you don't remember what's happened."

He'd asked me that before, and I wondered why this was such an important question.

"Or" he continued, "have you ever found clothes in your closet you don't remember buying? Does your handwriting or eyesight change?"

No therapist had ever asked me these kinds of questions, but I wanted to trust him, so I answered the best I could. "No, I just do compulsive things that embarrass me. I know it's me doing those things, but I feel… I feel out of control. Almost like— I don't know—like my mind turns off. When it's over, I tell myself I won't do it again. But I always do. Is that what you mean?"

"Not really. Multiplicity is more complicated than that."

"Multiplicity? I don't understand."

"You don't need to understand," he said, glancing at his watch. "We'll talk more later. And I'm increasing your meds."

He paused at the door. "Ah, one more thing. Have you ever seen the movie *Sybil* or *Three Faces of Eve?*"

"Only *Sybil.* I watched it on TV."

"Hmm," he muttered, then disappeared from the doorway.

Tears welled up in my eyes as I tugged at my hair. "Too much has happened, Baby. I don't know why I'm being asked these questions. They don't feel right and are not what I expected at all."

Dr. Braun believed that child sexual trauma was the root of multiple personalities long before I was admitted to the ward. Over the following weeks, I met two of his long-term, non-cult patients. Of the two, I liked Kathy the best. She told me about her many internal child personalities as if it were no big deal.

"All multiples have child parts," she said in a child's voice. "I'm Don." Then she switched back to her adult voice and added, "I also have twins, Connie and Nora. Connie is diabetic and Nora is not. Dr. Braun is trying to figure out how my body does that. But Connie doesn't like him, so she doesn't come out a lot."

I watched and learned from her. Kathy gave me a visual explanation of multiplicity and helped normalize my understanding of "parts" or personalities. All of Dr. Braun's patients learned from each other. His patients at the time were there because he wanted to create his own cult and multiplicity unit. It felt like we were enclosed in a giant mirror reflecting ourselves—words, hospital jargon, and concepts we'd never encountered before gradually entered our thoughts and behaviors. It was one huge toxic environment.

Dr. Braun believed that the mind's ability to "split" into new personalities supported his conspiracy theory that satanic cults were expanding worldwide. He told staff that cult leaders had powerful ways to program members, and if a part or alter revealed what they did in the cult, they had to kill themselves.

It was perfect. We, the "host," had little to no memories of abuse. Those memories were supposedly stored in one of our many alter personalities. We wouldn't start to remember what we did in the cult until we were hypnotized, drugged, and exposed to "recovered memory" therapy. The link between dissociative identity disorder and being a cult victim was seamless.

My long periods of silence, childlike behavior, and my ability to follow what my doctors suggested in a sand tray confirmed Braun's suspicions that I had been involved in cult activities and programmed to stay silent—or die.

Sometime after lunch, Dr. Bobbi came into my room. "Both Buddy and I think you should keep working in the sand. Someone is scheduled for today, so I'll set you up for tomorrow. Is that OK?"

"I guess," I said as she sat on my bed and took my hand.

"So, I'm curious. What did Dr. King say to you? Do you remember?"

"Sort of. She wanted to know if anyone in my family touched me the wrong way."

"Did they?" Bobbi asked.

"No," I said, slipping into child speech. "Nobodies did anyfing to me." But I stuttered, squeezing Dr. Bobbi's hand tight. "I just…"

"You just what, Linda?"

"Me's can't," I said. "Me's just can't."

"Can't what?"

"Me's can't tell you."

"OK, little one. Just know I'm here when you're ready. I need to check on another patient. I'll be back."

I was somewhat surprised and scared by how easily I could regress into childlike speech for long periods. But by the end of my three-month evaluation, switching effortlessly between adult and child became second nature. Eventually, this child part was given a name. She would serve as the dominant personality during my entire hospitalization—and stay with me for the rest of my life.

Dr. Bobbi had barely left the room when I started to feel the compulsive need for a sexual release. "Damn it, nothing's changed," I said as I paced and talked to the walls. "No one has asked me why I came here and waited for a truthful answer. All the team knows about me is what I tell Vicki during testing—and that's not a lot. All anybody wants to know is who's here and what my fingers have to say."

These sexual feelings were intense. Just like in the old days of my compulsive car rides, I needed my clothes off now. Not later, not in bed tonight. Now.

I knew afternoon rounds were over. Kate, my day nurse, and I had met during the morning. I didn't have a roommate, and five o'clock meds weren't due for another hour. I left my door open wide enough to be seen if someone passed by. Quickly, I removed my shoes and socks and made my way to my bed.

With eager hands, I yanked off my brown sweater, shirt, and bra. Within moments of removing my slacks and underwear, the room disappeared as snippets of sexual acts filled my mind and spread to my body. Within seconds, I achieved the orgasm I desired. The room blurred. My heart pounded in my ears as I curled my naked body into a fetal position. As my pulse slowed, tears suddenly rolled down my cheeks. "Damn it, why is it so damn hard to get help?"

It was a relief to feel the sexual energy fade away. Now my mind could focus on other things besides the pressure in my body and the hunger I couldn't control. It had been a long time since I'd experienced that immediate, compelling desire, and I was scared.

No, I told myself, don't go there yet. You're in the best hospital in Chicago, and so far, you've only hinted at what you've done. You need to find a way to get it all out and then see what happens.

I grabbed my clothes off my bed and floor and headed to my tiny, cramped bathroom. While pulling on clothes, the reality of what I had done hit me like a punch in the stomach. "Why," I screamed as I came out of the bathroom, "can't I goddamn control this?"

I heard a knock. "Shit." It was Dr. Bobbi.

"What can't you control, Linda? You look flushed. Are you OK?"

I shook my head no. There was no way I could tell her what I had just done. It was hard to breathe. It was hard to look at her, so I picked up Baby and said, "Me's can't say the words, but I think maybe Winda can white them on paper. Otay?"

"Sure," she said, looking deeper into my eyes. "Write if you can. I'll be back in twenty minutes."

I wrote, crossed out words, and wrote again. Finally, in uneven script, three short sentences appeared on a raggedly torn piece of paper:

I just took off all my clothes. I had a release. I wanted to be seen.

As she read, she let out the same audible sigh I'd heard in the sand room. Was she upset with me? Would she resign as my doctor and leave me only with Dr. Braun?

"Is me's in trouble?"

"No, cutie, you just have a whole lot of tough issues to work through." Sighing again, she said, "First, I want to have the adult Linda in this room."

This was the first time she asked for an adult. It took a moment, but I complied.

"Now, you need to know that desiring orgasm is normal, but it can't be done where you'll be seen. Understand?"

I nodded yes, while thinking, fat chance. That's not the way my compulsions work.

"Buddy and I have talked about your case, and we believe you have a lot to handle and deserve some privacy. So, you'll be moved to a private room as soon as one becomes available. We don't fully understand what's going on with you yet, but we're doing our best to figure it out."

"I don't know what's wrong with me either. That's why I'm here," I said, as fresh tears started to form. "Look," I said at last, "I still need to tell you some stuff."

"Like what?"

"Stuff about Dave and the sexual stuff I do, but as I told you before, I can't say some of the words."

"Can you write the words?"

"Maybe. Can we ask my fingers?"

"That might be helpful, but for now, why don't you try to write what you can't say? Also, no one will enter your room if your clothes are off. Does everyone inside understand?"

"Everyone inside? What does that mean?"

"It means horrible things have happened to you, and now you have lots of parts inside that help you cope."

"I just don't understand."

"You don't have to, Linda. All you need to know for now is that you're safe—and if you need to masturbate, please do it in the bathroom."

# Chapter 11

## *Life at Home*

The bathroom wasn't my preferred place to tend to my needs. I wished it were that simple, but the when and the why of taking off my clothes were far more complicated. The early days of marriage and my first lover, Raymond, came to mind. He started this whole damn thing, didn't he?

"You know," I said to Baby as I made myself comfortable on my hospital bed, "I was so sure I would settle down and be a real wife after Raymond was out of my life. But I was nowhere near ready for what was to come."

My mom never taught me the basics of cooking, and I hadn't remembered anything from home economics. I burned meals, cried, and ordered takeout. On Saturdays, Dave and I would drive to his parents' house, where I'd get a cooking lesson and listen to stories about the cabin in Wisconsin called OZ. Then I'd spend the rest of the week shopping and trying out new recipes.

We both got bicycles and rode around the neighborhood. It was fun to pick out homes we thought we'd like to live in. Dave would point to the big two-story houses while I pointed to the smaller, cozy ones. Married life felt like an ill-fitting garment I'd put on but couldn't take off.

My biggest problem was intimacy. I didn't know how to cuddle and couldn't appear naked in front of him. One morning, when I was in the shower, I heard, "Can I join you?"

"Dammit, no," I yelled, holding the plastic curtain's edge against the wall so he couldn't enter.

"Why not?"

My voice was shrill and echoed in the stall. "Dammit, Dave. Please. No."

His was a simple, acceptable request, but for the life of me, I could not say yes.

Every night I mentally drew a line down the middle of our queen-sized bed and slept as close to the edge as possible to avoid crossing it. Sex, when it happened, was quick and mechanical. There was no foreplay, warmth, or passion. No matter how many pep talks I gave myself, I couldn't let go and give him what I had so easily given to Raymond.

Raymond made me feel like I was no longer a child. He treated me like a desired, sexy woman, and I responded. My family and teachers said I was a nobody and would be a failure. Raymond treated me like someone worth noticing. I didn't have to be the "good girl" with Raymond.

Flirting and having sexual escapades in the middle of the warehouse excited me. Nothing felt taboo, and I loved the thrill and freedom of it all. Dave, however, made me feel like I was expected to be that "good girl" again. The exhilarating sense of freedom and excitement I'd felt with Raymond was now replaced by a deep aversion that affected every interaction I had with my husband.

I physically and emotionally couldn't bring myself to be with a man who knew from the start that I didn't want to marry him. I'd felt pressured to make a decision I wasn't ready for. I didn't love him, and I never once said, "I love you, Dave." It just wasn't there.

Even though I was making a mess of things as a frigid and distant wife, Dave felt we were ready to buy a home. He worked for an investment firm and was confident we could afford something small. We found our perfect two-bedroom ranch with a big fenced-in yard.

A few months later, a cocker-collie puppy joyfully ran through the garden I'd carefully planted with my favorite flowers. She was mostly white, with big copper-colored splotches on her ears and flanks. I named her Penny—the bright spot in my life. Finally, I could feel love, I thought, and she became my everything.

That fall, I started a job as a teacher's aide, which gave me the confidence to enroll in a child development program at our local junior college. The certificate wouldn't allow me to do much, but it was a start.

New neighbors, Mike and Deborah, who were about our age, moved in two doors down. They had a dog named Sadie and, like us, no children.

Deb taught first grade. Mike worked in insurance. We often gathered in one of our backyards on warm evenings and weekends. As the dogs played happily, Deb and I discussed books and classroom happenings, while the guys exchanged notes about their jobs. Those visits eventually became our Friday pizza-and-beer nights when winter arrived.

Deb was good for me. We both led busy lives, but she was always up for a quick visit. I told her about my mom and hinted that my marriage was shaky. She never pried, which I appreciated.

One Friday, Deb called. "Pizza tonight?"

"Sure. Same time?"

"Yep, we'll pick you up at six."

The tiny hole-in-the-wall restaurant felt like a second home. The smell of pizza greeted us as we stepped out of the car. The dim room was illuminated by votives in colored glass holders. Next to them were baskets of peanuts. When we arrived, the floor was already covered with shells.

The waitress came over. "You all want the usual?"

We all nodded in unison.

"Beer all around?"

"Coke for me," Deb replied with a smile.

I looked at her with a questioning glance.

"It looks like we're going to have a baby. It was confirmed today."

She caught me off guard, but I managed to say in a cheery voice, "Wow, that's great. I'm so happy for you."

And I was. But as drinks arrived, so did a memory.

I was a few days away from turning 12. It was almost Christmas, and Dad and I were heading to buy an aluminum Christmas tree from Polk Brothers. The car felt cold, and I was hugging myself to stay warm when, out of nowhere, he started talking.

"You know your mother cried and begged to come home after you were born. She wanted to be with the family on Christmas. She didn't seem to understand that the hospital required her to stay for three to five days. She cried a lot."

His voice trailed off, and I thought he was done. But he wasn't.

"And then, after your brother was born, I went through another rough patch with your mother. I didn't know how to help her. Do you remember anything about that time?"

"No," I'd softly replied. I was only three and a half then. "Why? Am I supposed to remember something?"

"No, not really. But I see so much of your mother in you. I worry about you, that's all."

Once again, I felt like I'd grown up at the wrong time. Postpartum depression and psychosis were not well-researched or understood in the '40s and '50s.

Mom was 20 when she married my 21-year-old dad. They planned to live with her parents while their dream home was being built. Three months later, Dad was called to serve in the army. He returned a year later, and within three months, Mom was pregnant with me. Their house wouldn't be ready for another year, so when she brought me home from the hospital, she handed me off to my grandmother.

I never truly bonded with Mom. She couldn't give me what I

needed to feel safe, wanted, and secure. I carried this inability to connect—along with the fear that I might develop postpartum depression if I ever got pregnant—into my marriage. When I wondered if I could love and care for a baby, my honest answer was always *no.*

Dave and I never really talked. From the beginning, we didn't plan vacations, discuss our hopes and dreams for the future, or ask ourselves if we wanted children. We didn't consider names or timing or what kind of parents we might be.

Instead of being honest about my true feelings, I buried them and went through the motions of wanting children, while secretly hoping—God forbid—that it would never happen.

As months went by without pregnancy, I read books on how to start a family. I took my temperature and followed every bit of advice they gave. Then I had a procedure to check if my ovaries were healthy. Dave also had himself evaluated. We both proved to have no physical issues.

I don't remember whose idea it was to try artificial insemination, but I do recall feeling a huge internal conflict. I was very aware of how my anger and instability might affect an innocent child's life.

Yet one day, I found myself on a cold exam table, waiting for Dave to do his part in the tiny office bathroom. I was nervous that the insemination would work and I'd become the mother I feared I might be. There were no cuddles afterward. There was no "Darling, I hope this works" talk.

It was too early to expect changes in my body, but I still spent the month searching for them. When my period started, I waited for tears to come. They didn't.

What came instead was an enormous sense of relief.

Afterward, I knew there wouldn't be a second try. I was done. I couldn't love Dave, and I couldn't conceive a baby. I felt like I was failing as a woman—which did nothing to boost my self-esteem or make my marriage more bearable.

# Chapter 12

## *Reaching Out for Help*

After Deb's baby announcement, I focused more on my marriage. I placed flowers from the garden on the dinner table and asked more questions about my husband's work. When Dave wanted to go for a bike ride, I said, "Sure, that sounds like fun."

Agreeing to have sex was harder, but when asked, I didn't pull away. We smiled more and started going out for dinner and a movie on Saturday nights. It wasn't a perfect marriage—I still held back and knew I didn't love Dave—but he wasn't complaining or asking for more. I began to think maybe we could make our marriage work.

One afternoon, as I was dusting and thinking about what to make for dinner, this thought popped into my mind: I wonder what it would feel like to take my blouse off and ride in the car topless?

I was stunned. I had a vivid imagination and a rich fantasy world, but I'd never thought of anything like that before. I couldn't even say the word "breast" when I was younger, and I still avoided it during my annual exams.

And now, I thought, you want to know what it might feel like to drive around topless?

Yes, my body told me—loud and clear. Yes, oh yes.

Like the bees drawn to the flowers in my garden, my body felt driven. The thought wouldn't leave me alone. The idea quickly grew.

I wasn't aware at the time that what I was going through was my first exhibitionist episode. I also didn't realize that exhibitionism was a legitimate disorder—and that, with proper counseling, I could have gotten the help I needed. Eventually, the exhibitionism turned into hypersexuality.

Within minutes of that absurd thought, I found myself dressed in shorts and a sleeveless button-down blouse. I headed toward the garage door and sat in the driver's seat. As I took off my blouse and bra, I felt the sexual tension build. It was intense. I didn't want to release it too soon, so I placed my bra on the passenger seat and put my blouse back on, leaving it unbuttoned. I needed to hold onto this excitement as long as possible.

We lived near a major expressway, and as I approached the entrance ramp, I turned up the air, made sure the doors were locked, and pulled my blouse wide open. As I drove, my body craved more. I lost track of time and space, removed my blouse with one hand, yanked down my shorts below my belly, and sped up to pass the next semi.

The first run was an incredible high—beyond any feeling I'd experienced with Raymond. I thought I could fly. There was no here, no there, no sense of danger or getting caught. I was just one gigantic fireball of energy. That is, until I had the desired orgasm—and the high was gone. Then I couldn't get home fast enough.

I used the remote and pulled into the garage. Like a zombie, I headed for the bedroom. Naked from the waist up, I grabbed winter clothes from dresser drawers. Quickly, I slipped my arms into a flannel shirt and a long-sleeved cardigan. I pulled sweatpants over my shorts and slid wool socks onto my feet. I needed clothes on my body. The more, the better.

What I'd done felt wrong. The thrill of being seen while

exposing myself—and getting away with it—was gone. Over time, I'd learn that my compulsions brought extreme highs, and when they ended, as they always did, those feelings of ecstasy were replaced with shame, guilt, and a never-ending promise never to do it again.

I was sure other women didn't do what I did. I knew people cut themselves, drank, did drugs, or gambled, but I'd never heard stories about dangerous sexual desires and urges. I knew men cheated on their wives and exposed themselves to unsuspecting women. But women didn't cheat on their husbands, nor did they drive semi-naked in their cars—did they?

I felt so conflicted. How could something feel so good and at the same time cause so much torment? Still in a daze, I grabbed a stuffed animal and my favorite afghan. While sobbing, I called Penny and, with my arms wrapped around her, curled into a fetal position on the bed.

I knew how to take care of my own sexual needs. Masturbating was a normal part of my daily routine. But what had just happened didn't feel like anything I recognized. I didn't understand why I felt the need to drive down the highway half-naked in plain sight of truckers while having an orgasm.

That summer, I made myself the standard promise: this was a one-time thing and wouldn't happen again. But it wasn't. The blare of an occasional truck horn, paired with my need for those dangerous highs, lured me back to the expressway two to three times a week. I'd been seen—and that feeling made me yearn for more.

This was dangerous, but I was lucky. Only one driver ever followed me off my exit. Even though I was able to lose him in traffic, my heart pounded as I took a long, circuitous way home.

That incident made me stop and think. I realized I was no longer safe from harm. But my exhibitionist thoughts offered no relief. They escalated, promising that if I drove naked while masturbating, my highs would be even more intense. And they were.

On one of my last rides, I missed my exit. Confused, I took the next one but didn't know where I was. Panic set in as I tried to orient myself—naked—in local traffic. No street signs made sense. I scrunched down as low as I could in the driver's seat.

I managed to get home safely, but as I hurriedly pulled on multiple layers of clothes, I realized, without a doubt, that I needed help before I got arrested for indecent exposure—or caused an accident.

I looked through the yellow pages twice. I thought telling a female therapist what I was doing would be easier than telling a man, but none were listed in my area. I was disappointed. It had to be a man—or no one at all. And no one wasn't an option. I knew I needed therapy.

I wasn't sure what to expect, so I was relieved when Tom, my new therapist, greeted me at the door and brought me into a small, cozy room. I looked around and chose a chair as far away from him as I could.

He didn't start by asking what had brought me there, which I appreciated. Instead, he said he liked clients to share their stories and believed that what they needed to work on would become clear. That felt doable. It gave me a chance to talk about my family and how I'd grown up. These weren't light topics, but they were easier to discuss than my marriage, Raymond, or my car rides.

There were other words besides "breast" I couldn't say —"penis," "orgasm," "masturbation"—they never came out of my mouth. Yet somehow, I had to find a way to say them, because what I was doing was slowly eating me alive.

After nearly two months, I was still hesitant to talk to Tom about my marriage. My promise to fulfill Dave's requests for sex had once again faded. I knew this was linked to my anxiety about my car rides.

My affair, combined with those drives, left me devoid of self-respect. Somehow, I thought that if I allowed myself to have sex with Dave, he'd realize what I had done behind his back. I knew that didn't make sense, but guilt and shame played tricks on my mind. They told me I'd never be able to keep my promises—and that I didn't deserve a man as kind as Dave.

Every week, I promised myself I'd tell Tom what was really going on, but I'd chicken out at the last moment. I'd go for another highway run and watch as a driver honked and pointed toward the exit. Finally, I decided I had to tell Tom the whole story. Today was the day.

"What's the topic for today?" Tom asked.

"I have to tell you something."

"OK, I'm listening."

"Well… I take my clothes off in my car," I whispered, "while I drive around."

"You do?" he asked, leaning forward. "Tell me more."

But I couldn't. Fear hit me like a tornado, twisting and turning in my gut. It swirled through my body, then left—taking all my words with it.

Tom tried again. "Can you tell me how you feel when you do that?"

With silent tears, I shook my head no.

"Try," he said.

I wanted to scream. I'm driving naked while I masturbate and I'm terrified! But I remained frozen, unable to say the words that held me hostage.

Tom tried several times to get me to talk, but I couldn't even say my name. That day, my session ended early. Tom called me the next day to check on me. I told him I was fine. And I was— until the night, a few weeks later, when Dave had had enough.

"Dave lost his temper with me," I said when I arrived for my session.

"What happened?"

"We were about to go to bed when Dave came out of the bathroom naked. He asked me to take off my nightgown, which I couldn't do. He said, 'Come on, Linda, I need you.'"

"I just couldn't make myself do it," I said. "And I said no."

Tom remained quiet, watching me struggle for control.

"And then Dave slammed his fist against the wall. I heard it crack, and he yelled, 'Dammit, Linda, we've been married over three years, and I've never seen you naked. You refuse sex, and you don't talk to me. What the hell is wrong with you?'"

"And I couldn't answer him, Tom. Because I don't know what's wrong with me either. That's one of the reasons I'm here."

"He didn't hurt you, did he?" Tom asked.

"No, he just scared me. He was so angry," I said, biting my lip. "Dave went back to the bathroom, and I left for the couch. This marriage isn't good for either of us."

"I can see that now," Tom said. "I'm sorry that happened. But, on the other hand, this gives us a behavior to work on."

# Chapter 13

*True Confessions*

I couldn't stop smiling the day my child development certificate arrived in the mail. I had proven to myself that I could handle college coursework. Dave and Deb congratulated me and agreed we should all go to a fancy restaurant to celebrate with something other than pizza.

"If you want to be more than just an aide, you should consider going for your associate of arts degree," Deb said when we were alone. "Once you have that piece of paper, you can be a preschool teacher and maybe, if you want, have a career."

Deb didn't go back to her job after her baby was born. We didn't talk as often as we used to, but when she could, she'd put the baby in his carrier, and we'd all go out for pizza.

I wanted my associate degree, so I re-entered junior college and started taking the classes I needed. Dave was glad I decided to go back to school. When I explained how my high school counselor told me I wasn't college material, Dave tried hard to support me, and I tried just as hard to accept his kindness. But we didn't have a marriage. We were two people living under one roof, each leading our own separate lives.

Dave and I had now been married nearly five years. I had a job I enjoyed and would receive my associate degree in child development at the end of the year. In my mind, this was my first step toward asking for a divorce.

But I thought a divorce wouldn't help me control my sexual urges. I was seriously flirting with a guy in my music theory class. He reminded me of the early days with Raymond, and that was risky. I needed an intervention, so I scheduled an emergency session with Tom. Today, I decided, was the day I would finally come clean.

"So, do you want to tell me what this is all about?" Tom asked after I sat down. "You look like you're ready to explode."

After a few false starts, everything spilled out, like someone finally lifted the gates of a dam. Raymond and the car rides were the hardest topics to discuss.

"Have you had more affairs?"

Yes, a few, which is why I'm here. I don't understand why I can give myself to strangers but not to my husband. And now there's this guy at school who reminds me of Raymond, and I don't want to have another affair, but my body does.

"Please, I need help!"

I waited and held my breath as the room spun. What would he think? Would he understand?

"OK, I hear you, and you're right. You do need help. I'm just a social worker, so I suggest scheduling a session with my colleague, a psychiatrist. I'll update him on what you told me and recommend an evaluation. How does that sound?"

"Scary," I said, holding my breath again.

"Yes, but what you're doing right now is also scary. Let's see if we can get some answers."

The evaluation occurred the following week. I was greeted by a man in a white coat who spoke so softly I thought something was wrong with my ears. He took notes and nodded as he collected my family history. Then, after administering a Rorschach test, he said, "Tom filled me in on your case, but I'd like you to tell me what's going on."

You know my marriage isn't going well. I never wanted to get married in the first place, but when I told my soon-to-be husband and my parents I didn't want to marry, everyone made a big deal out of it. Now I feel stuck. But I'm working on a preschool degree to maybe help me get out of the marriage.

"Is that all?"

"No. I'm also having affairs with men I don't know well or… not at all."

My stomach turned, so as quickly as I could gather my thoughts, I said, "And I used to take off all my clothes and drive down the expressway. And I want to do it again."

I held my breath, watched his face, and waited for his response. And this doctor, dressed in his white coat, smiled and replied, "I bet the truck drivers must've loved seeing you like that."

Stunned, I slowly exhaled and looked back at him with wide eyes. You bastard. Can't you hear the pain in my voice and see my flushed face? Don't you understand? What kind of response is that to someone who's here for help?

Immediately, I felt a huge wall of distrust slam into me and shut me down. There was so much more I wanted to say, but I couldn't trust this man with anything. All I wanted was to vomit all over his shiny black shoes.

With an eerie calmness, I said, "I'm not feeling well. I need to leave."

As I gathered my things, he handed me prescriptions for lithium and Valium.

"I'll be in touch with Tom," he said. It took everything in me not to slam the door when I left.

On Tom's recommendation, I had the prescription filled. The lithium didn't touch my compulsions, and the Valium—tranquilizer of choice in the early 70s—only made me feel like the world was made of rubber. I saved those for when I wanted to zone out.

I never told Tom what happened during my humiliating consultation with his colleague. I'd felt betrayed by his referral and decided I could no longer trust him to help me, so one day, after an unproductive session, I left his office and never returned. I left therapy.

Looking back, I realize I didn't lack trust in Tom—I lacked trust in myself. I hadn't developed the sense of self needed to stand up for what I wanted and needed. Part of it was the culture I grew up in, and part of it was being taught, by a look or silence, not to ask questions or disobey authority. The only thing I knew how to do was be a "good girl." I was so terrified of being called dumb and being made to feel less than that I blindly followed what I was told to do, whether it was in my best interest or not.

I was thankful, though, to have those prescriptions on hand, because Dave and I were moving into our newly built tri-level home. It was Dave's idea to move; he still wanted his big house. I reluctantly agreed, and while it was fun to pick out the features we wanted, there were many disagreements. I didn't like change, nor did I like leaving the convenience of living so close to Deb. She was the only real friend I had. But on the plus side, we would no longer be living near an expressway.

Once we were settled in our new home, I made six new rules for myself: no sexual escapades, be kind to Dave, keep my temper in check, act like a married woman, love my new home, graduate from junior college. The only rule I followed was graduating from junior college. By fall, I was hired at a local preschool and planned to make it my career, but when the school owners decided to move to Florida and close the school at the end of that year, my career plans ended.

I was disappointed, but it motivated me to apply to a four-year college. I'd become an elementary school teacher, earn a decent salary, and then work toward divorcing Dave.

College was helpful. Dave and I argued less when my weekends were filled with homework. With me busy, Dave would go hunting with friends. This was my favorite time. It was just Penny and me.

I found the magazines one weekend. I'd just finished hanging the last of Dave's shirts when my eyes flicked to the top shelf and saw the words *Playboy* and *Penthouse*. I'd seen those titles in the bookstores I frequented, but I'd never dared to open one.

As I pulled the top one off the shelf, my eyes caught a glamorous, scantily clad woman. For a moment, she reminded me of the calendars hanging on the back of the door in the water company warehouse. I longed for that innocent time but understood those days were gone. Still, as I flipped through the pages and felt the inner heat rise, I knew I'd discovered a new way to fuel my fantasies.

# Chapter 14

## *The Last Straw*

Dave now came home from work to silence.

"Hi, hon. I'm home," he'd call as he came in from the garage. When there was no reply, I'd hear him talk to himself as he climbed the stairs.

"Hi Dave, how was your day? Great. How was yours ...?"

That hurt. I could hear the words I should be saying to welcome him home, but I could not make them come out of my mouth.

I slept every night on the couch. While all was quiet, I could hear him in the bathroom talking with his imaginary woman while he turned the pages of the same porn magazine I looked at during the day.

It was a miserable way for both of us to live. I didn't have a job and, even if I did, I had no credit in my name. While it wasn't right, I took all my anger and frustration out on Dave.

Deb's second child was a girl. Her eyes were deep china blue, her hair, brown ringlets, and I wanted her for my own. I was thrilled when Deb asked us to be the baby's godparents. Having a goddaughter would be the best of all worlds. I could fuss over her and someone else would raise her.

It was the end of another ordinary pizza night. Dave, Deb, and I were in the kitchen doing last-minute cleanup when I noticed Mike putting his finger to his lips and gesturing for me to join him in the front room.

"Are you going to be home on Monday?" he whispered, glancing towards the kitchen. "I have a client out your way and thought I'd stop by to say hi."

"I guess," I whispered back. "What time?"

"Not sure. Afternoon. OK?"

I knew by his lowered voice this was for my ears only.

I was confused. Jackets and goodbyes had started. There was no way to ask more questions.

On our way home, I searched my mind. Did Mike ever flirt with me before? Had I missed something? We'd never been alone with each other. We saw each other on pizza nights. That was it.

Warring thoughts continuously ran across my mind that entire weekend.

OK, you're pretty sure Mike wants some action with you. What are you going to do when he rings your doorbell?

I don't know.

Do you find him attractive?

No, he's blah.

Then why would you even consider doing something risky with him?

He's a man and it's expected, isn't it? It feels like all I'm good for is a quickie with whoever wants it. Intercourse doesn't mean anything to me. It's messy and takes too long. Don't you understand, I thought to myself, I don't want to be doing these things? When it's over, I hate myself.

Then why'd you keep doing it?

Even though I'm sick with guilt and shame after it's all over, at the time, it's sexy and daring and just thinking about what I'm going to do excites me.  Can you say no to Mike?

He's your goddaughter's dad, my thoughts whispered a few hours later. Doesn't that mean anything to you?

It does. That baby is my heart. Just be a good girl and say thanks for stopping by, but no thank you.

Deb is my only friend and I'm not going to do anything with her husband and that's final.

No therapist had talked to me about how the body reacts when it's aroused. I was not told that wanting and needing intimacy was normal. My mom told me I was abnormal because I didn't date or talk about boys and I had a crush on my female art teacher. And I believed her.

No one knew how scared and out of control I felt. On Monday, my mind continued to torment me. I dusted and flipped through a *Good Housekeeping* magazine. Maybe, I thought, he won't show, and all of this anxiety will be for nothing.

It was two in the afternoon when the doorbell rang, and I could still hear myself trying to say no.

Opening the door, I felt like both of us were experiencing the same moment of decision.

After a brief hesitation and silence, we climbed the stairs and headed towards the couch. Our conversation started with the usual niceties.

"How are you? Nice weather, huh?"

I answered and waited. Then it came.

"What would you like me to do to you?"

"Well, you could fuck my tits."

Mike smiled and agreed.

The next thing I remember is staring at his penis between my breasts and wondering why this act looked so sexy in the magazine. I was grossed out and felt nothing. It was then, in this total lack of excitement, that I realized I was making the biggest mistake of my life.

It was over before I reached an orgasm. He asked if he could help with that. I shook my head no.

In silence, I watched him dress, afraid I would completely fall apart if I moved. He asked if we could do this again sometime. I kept my silence.

I did not walk him to the door, and it was only when I heard it snap shut that I fully released my breath. My mind was in a million places. There were no take backs or do-overs. What had I done? Half-naked, I poured my first glass of wine and went to where my fix lay waiting for me on the top shelf. I flipped the pages, gulped down the wine, poured another and chose a photo and story that didn't resemble what I'd just experienced. My release came quickly and brought the surge of tears and waves of deep sadness I was holding back. It was over, but this time, I found no comfort or peace in the pile of clothes I'd put on my body. Clothes usually dulled the shame. This time, it didn't work. I'd gone too far.

I didn't think this situation could get worse, but it did. I kept a journal hidden in a desk drawer in my office. What had transpired between Mike and me was one of the things I wrote about after my third glass of wine.

The next afternoon, the phone rang. It was Deb. "I know what you did with my husband." Her voice was as cold as ice. "Our friendship is over. I never want to see you again! Ever!"

My mind spun. How did Deb find out? Mike wouldn't tell her, would he? My heart raced as I fled to the bathroom and threw up.

When Dave came home that night, I told him I was sick. "Probably the flu," I said. He was kind and left me alone.

Four days later, he was waiting for me when I returned from the store. "I know," he said, handing me my diary. "I know everything."

I was surprised at how calm I was. Detached from my body and reality, I told Dave the journal entry was made up, something I only wanted to happen. He silently watched my performance, picked up his car keys, and left. I never knew what made Dave search my desk drawers or what else he had read. I was too shocked to ask. The days after were unspeakably challenging. I ripped up every journal and personal paper I could lay my hands on while Dave spent time in his room with the door closed, ignoring me.

We both were guarded when we finally came out from our safe corners. Meals slowly went from silent to polite. We were back together and still oceans apart. I could tell as he watched me suspiciously when I came home from anywhere that all trust was broken. We danced around each other as if doing an ill-choreographed rumba.

One morning, while drinking a cup of coffee that had gone cold, I thought, What if my sexual behavior is the result of my having multiple personalities? It was a crazy, impossible idea, and I knew I was self-diagnosing. But what could it hurt? At least I'd have an answer.

I watched the movie *Sybil* and couldn't shake it off. My mom wasn't as bad as Sybil's mom. Still, when Sybil switched personalities, I felt I could relate to her.

If I had known that Sybil did not have multiple personalities and that her book and the movie would eventually be largely discredited, my life might have taken a completely different direction. Sybil was simply another confused woman attempting to satisfy her therapist. Like me, she had fallen victim to an unethical system where the allure of fame and money outweighed the value of an individual's life.

But at the time, I thought, Okay, okay, I just can't live like this anymore. I really need to call someone, and if it turns out that I have multiple personalities, I'll have my answer. If not, then I can cross that off my list of possibilities.

Before I could change my mind, I picked up the phone and dialed 411 directory assistance. "Hi, I'm looking for the name of a doctor in the Chicago area who knows about multiple personalities."

"One moment, please. I will check."

"Yes, there is just one. Dr. Bennett G. Braun is a certified psychiatrist, and his office is located in the downtown area. Would you like the number?"

"Yes, please," I said.

I had the number. Now, to gather the courage and make the call.

Had I not seen that movie on TV, in my moment of desperation, I might never have reached out to Dr. Braun.

"I did make the call though," I whispered to Baby. And look where it got us.

# Chapter 15

## *Transfer and Hypnosis*

While sucking my thumb, dressing Baby and myself in matching colors, and waiting for the transfer to a private room, I wrote in detail about all the compulsive things I did. It was difficult. My own words and experiences sparked intense sexual tension within me. How could something I couldn't discuss hold so much power? I wondered this as I took care of my body's needs under the bed covers between the nurse's rounds. Fears that I'd never leave my marriage, never experience real intimacy, and that I would always be battling my compulsive behaviors were my constant companions.

After Dave read my journal, I never thought I could share my writings with anyone. Letting Dr. Bobbi read my journal was a big step, but I was sure that once she read the words I'd agonized over, I'd find my answers.

"I wrote what you asked for," I told Dr. Bobbi before leaving for the sand tray room. "Here's my journal. It's all there." I looked for a reaction on her face, but there was none.

I waited for days, but she never commented or asked for further clarification. I found this odd, but I figured there was still time. After all, I still had nearly two months before my promised diagnosis.

The room transfer happened after a breakfast I barely touched. My day nurse, Kate, knocked loudly and then entered my room with two new hospital bracelets.

"Here you go," she said, pushing up the sleeve of my brown sweater and attaching one to my left wrist. "You need to wear a bracelet at all times."

"Baby has it," I said.

"Yes. We noticed, so now she has one of her own. I'll let you put it on her." It read *Baby Cooper.* "Staff will be in soon to help you move."

It didn't take more than five minutes to move my modest belongings into the room on the side of the building that offered a perfect view of the Congress Expressway. A long window with steel bars stretched along the outer wall of the small room. A ten-foot fake marble ledge protruded below. A black pull rod hung from the right side to draw the unattractive plastic-lined drapes.

Kate opened my drawer and started to refold some of the clothes that had fallen along the way. "Please leave my clothes alone. I need to put my own things away, by myself," I said, as a feeling of irritation began to build up.

"OK," Kate said, starting to leave. "I'll be back later to discuss why you're not attending community meetings."

"I'm not going to any more community meetings."

Struggling to stay in control, I swallowed and said, in a voice I used at home with Dave when I got angry, "I've been to at least four meetings and they're all a complete waste of time. Everyone spaces out and asks the same damn questions over and over. I know how to get clean sheets and towels. I know how to do laundry and get snacks. So, I'm not going." I lowered my voice a bit. "It's just—you feel like my mom wanting to control my life. I still have the right to put my clothes away, don't I?"

At that moment, I hated her, hated this new room, and hated life itself. Besides, I thought I might miss Dr. Bobbi if she came by.

"Who's here?" Kate asked.

I stopped cold.

"Me?"

"Well, I've never heard you use that tone of voice before. We'll discuss this later."

"Whatever," I mumbled, then thought, I can't blame her. How would she know how I sounded at home when my temper got the best of me? This was the first time since I'd set foot on the ward that I'd heard or seen even a ghost of the person I used to be.

While arranging Baby's clothes in the vanity, I pulled out the Gideon Bible and tossed it under my bed. Then, while I was at it, I stood on the lone chair in the room and unhooked the tarnished Christian cross from above the dresser. That, too, was flung under the bed. I planned to put everything back when I left, but until then, I had no room for God.

As I calmed down and set my toiletries by the sink, I finally smiled. Nobody would be moving them. I was alone, and any mess I made would be mine. I had just placed my bag of art supplies on my tray table when I heard a loud knock.

"I see you're all settled in," Dr. Braun said. "Dr. Bobbi and I met with your team this morning and discussed your progress. There are still many unanswered questions about what's going on with you. We've agreed that while I'm your primary doctor, I'll only see you twice a week. Dr. Bobbi will have sessions with you every day. I've also increased your Inderal and added a mood stabilizer."

Still feeling argumentative, I glared at him. "I don't like meds."

"It's not about what you like," he said, moving his face closer to mine. "It's what you need. The Inderal helps with switching parts." I felt like Braun was trying to goad me into accepting his med increase, which made me even more defiant.

I pursed my lips and replied, "I didn't have parts when I came here. Why are you telling me I have them now?"

Dr. Braun continued as if I hadn't spoken. "I'm keeping an

open mind after the incident in your room, your ongoing periods of silence and thumb sucking, and Kate now noting that you showed a side of yourself she's never seen before. Let me just say I have my suspicions."

Then, getting up to leave, he said, "Staff has been instructed to knock loudly before they enter. Have a good day."

"You know, Baby, maybe asking for a doctor who knew about multiplicity was not such a great idea. Dr. Braun scares me. A lot!"

I glanced at my watch. It was now 10 a.m. The sand tray room was reserved for 10:30. But where was Dr. Bobbi? I wouldn't be going anywhere until I saw her.

"Sorry, sorry," she said, rushing in. "Another patient was in crisis. I see Baby is right where she belongs. How about giving me a hug?"

"A hug?"

"You do know how to hug, don't you?"

I tried to remember when I'd had my last hug. Coming up blank, I shook my head no.

"Come here, cutie," she said with a smile that lit up her blue eyes. "Let me show you how it's done."

I quickly stepped into her open arms, and as I was enveloped by her slippery red-and-black blouse, the lines between doctor and patient started to blur. She smelled like sheets hung out to dry in the sizzling summer sun. She held me tightly, pulling me close, gently rocking me back and forth, then let me go. "That's how it's done in my world. Next time, I'll teach you how to give kisses on both my cheeks."

Never in my life had I felt such a powerful presence. Without words, in that moment, this "doctor" became the mother I always wished for and the woman I would come to love deeply. One instant she had the ability to make me feel like a vulnerable three-year-old, and the next she awakened a desire and need in me that I couldn't explain. No matter how complicated and dark our path became, I would follow this woman wherever she led.

I picked up Baby, closed the door, and headed to the sand tray room. I passed a room where an elderly woman in a faded pink nightgown shouted, "Nurse, nurse, help me, help me, someone pleeeeease help me!" I squeezed Baby tighter and hurried past her door.

I was growing more comfortable in the sand tray room. It was small, quiet, and had a reassuring routine. There was something freeing about picking up a figure representing someone or something and placing it in the sand. In the days and years ahead, my trays would feel like I was creating visual scenes from a story in my mind, and, in a way, I was. But it wasn't a true story; it was one being fed to me, detail by detail, by doctors with an agenda.

Time slipped away, and when I stepped back from my tray, I saw my mom and dad standing next to objects that showed their favorite hobbies. There were also many cars and a red truck. Rows of trees with yellow plastic eyes lined the edge.

It took years for me to realize that, back then, my mind was trying to portray what I did during my marriage: sex in cars, trucks, behind bushes, in the open air—always worried someone might see me and report me to the police. How different my life could have been if only the right questions had been asked about these early experiences.

Having me build in the sand tray was truly an experiment on Dr. Bobbi's part—an experiment that, unfortunately for myself and others, worked in her favor. By the end of my four years, Dr. Bobbi, who had no training in sand tray therapy, would use sections of my tray to produce a training film for therapists on how to use this technique with ritual abuse clients. These trays, wrongly used to "remember" what was never done, would damage many lives, as they also provided information that could be used against us. While in sand tray sessions, I often heard, "But in your previous tray you told me . . ."

Both doctors came into my room around dinnertime. I wondered what was wrong and grabbed Baby for comfort.

"You're OK," Dr. Bobbi said. "Dr. Braun and I want to see what your unconscious mind has to say about the tray you built this afternoon." She sat on my bed and placed her finger in the middle of my forehead. "Now close your eyes and go inside. Ten, nine . . ."

The first voice I heard was Dr. Braun's.

"I have a few questions I need to ask you before Dr. Bobbi asks hers. Has anyone inside ever participated in any kind of ritual that involved hurting animals?"

"No?" I said, faltering. I'd heard his words, but they made no sense. Why was I being asked about hurting animals?

"Do you or someone inside have secrets?"

Secrets? "Some," I mumbled while thinking, who doesn't have secrets?

"I thought so," I heard him say. "Have you or anyone inside ever been to Pitcairn, Pennsylvania?"

"I think maybe we went through Pennsylvania once during a vacation."

"That's all I need to know for now," he said.

The voice changed. Now it was Dr. Bobbi's. "Now everybody listen. Does anyone know someone by the name of Margo from Pitcairn?"

"I don't think so."

"Did your family travel a lot?"

"Mostly during the summer?"

"You're doing well," Dr. Bobbi said. "I have one last question. In the tray today, you had lots of cars and a camera next to your father. Did your father ever take pictures of you?"

Yes, of course he did, I thought. He took pictures of everything. Then I wondered where this session was going. What was I supposed to say?

I wanted to explain this was Dad's hobby, just like my mom's was drawing and painting. How much did a person say when they were hypnotized? Was I even hypnotized? Would Dr. Bobbi be mad at me if I wasn't? My eyes were closed, so my radar felt off. It was hard to see visual cues, which made me panic.

Not waiting for my first reply, Dr. Bobbi asked a second

question. "Did your father take pictures of you without your clothes on?"

This time, my body stiffened and heated up as my fingers moved rapidly in the air. Whenever I felt scared or frustrated, I often used my hands to communicate. However, instead of being seen as my way of expressing myself, my team interpreted these gestures as me flashing cult symbols. When I said my movements weren't signals, I wasn't believed.

I didn't know how to answer Dr. Bobbi's question inside her other question. Yes, Dad took pictures of me. But no, I always had clothes on. These questions felt confusing. So, covering all my bases, I said, "Yes. No. Maybe?"

"It's OK," I heard her say. "That's a hard thing to admit."

"Now I will count, and when I reach ten, you will be back in the room."

Dr. Braun wasn't there when I opened my eyes. Dr. Bobbi was still on my bed.

"What was that all about?" I asked in a voice that was half mine. "Me's didn't feel like I was hypnotized, and me's don't know anything about hurting animals or habing secrets, and my daddy woved takin pitures of wots of things."

"You might not know some of these answers, Linda, but Buddy and I believe there's a good chance someone inside does."

That day, the innocent placement of cars and a camera next to my dad was used to prove that I'd experienced home abuse and had traveled out of state with my family to cult meetings. I grew to dislike the words "close and go inside" because they implied I was supposed to calm my mind and let the truth come out from within. But the truth was, I didn't understand their strange, leading questions, and there was nothing calm about going inside. Their questions only made me face the fear of making a mistake when I answered. My mind would spin in circles until I just blurted out whatever made-up details made the most sense to me. I hoped I wouldn't be proven wrong.

Maybe I was more hypnotized than I thought. Still, I realize now that I couldn't have said anything wrong. The main goal of those hypnosis sessions was to plant names and suggestions about cults into my drug-filled mind. Unfortunately, it worked. Within days, a crude scene of an animal sacrifice would start to form in my mind.

# Chapter 16

## *A Trip to the Gift Shop*

While reading a chapter from *The World of Pooh* to Baby a few days later, I heard "Code blue, code blue" echoing down the hospital corridors. I put my book down and popped my head out the door. "This must be something big," I said to Baby. "There's a lot of staff rushing down the hall."

I wasn't sure what was happening, so I sat back on my bed and finished reading the story about Kanga and Roo. Then I opened my journal and started writing it was time to get in touch with Dave, even though I didn't want to.

Journal writing was essential. It helped me keep track of my daily experiences. As more pills were added to my small white cup, I grew more anxious about forgetting important details. I wrote about everything from the ordinary— "For breakfast I had . . ."— to the profound— "This morning I took my clothes off and let my imagination carry me past the stale smells and constant noise of the ward."

Everything about my so-called therapy was unconventional. Eventually, Dr. Bobbi said she enjoyed reading my journal entries. I asked her if we could discuss the entry about my compulsions and marriage. She assured me we would, but we never did. I didn't get the chance to talk about anything that truly mattered to me, not even my troubled marriage.

During the day, I felt more tired and had difficulty concentrating. Details from the previous day were blurry and harder to remember. Dr. Braun said that was normal and that as my body adjusted to the prescribed medications, those symptoms would fade.

Nights also became more difficult as I found it increasingly hard to fall asleep. Every night, at the top of the hour, a nurse would check on each patient. They'd shine a light into the room and quietly call "rounds," then mark on a clipboard whether each patient was awake or asleep. There was nothing I could control during the day, but I thought I could at least let the nurse know when I was awake by calling out "squares." It was a silly thing to do, but I was grabbing onto anything I could control—or that would give me solid proof if I were asked, "How many times do you wake during the night?"

When I finally fell asleep, I would have the same childhood dreams about tornadoes coming down the road to swallow me up. I dreaded those dreams when I was young, and I dreaded them even more now. They seemed to mirror the growing fear that, little by little, my mind was being destroyed.

Dr. Bobbi usually checked in with me when she arrived on the ward, but she was very late that morning during the code blue. After our hug and cheek kisses, she said, "You wrote in your journal yesterday that you wanted to get out of here, so I was wondering if you'd like to come with me to the hospital gift shop?"

"Really?"

"Yes, but you have to do one thing for me."

Skeptical, I said, "What?"

"You will need to leave Baby in your room."

"Why?"

"Because it's time for you to go places without her, and this will be an excellent way to practice."

Hesitating while looking at Baby, Dr. Bobbi added, "We could also go for ice cream in the small dining area. How does that sound?"

I rubbed my hands down my sides and took one more look at Baby. "Otay."

"Here we go," she said, taking my hand. "Off to the gift shop we go, hi-ho."

It took a few minutes to adjust. As we got off the elevator, I felt like I was walking on the slanted floors of a funhouse. I almost tripped over my own feet, so Dr. Bobbi slowed down and asked, "How's it going?"

"The floors keep moobing, and it's so bright, and it's hard to breathe."

"Ah, well, you haven't been outside the ward since you arrived, so that will even out soon. I'm right here, and you're doing fine. However, it will be better for you if you can get an adult out here."

By now, the mention of parts and "finding an adult" was no longer foreign to me. I didn't exactly know what all that meant, but I knew how to comply with the request.

By the time we reached the gift shop, some of the adult me had returned and was taking in the many fall decorations. Pumpkins and a basket of fake apples sat next to a friendly-looking scarecrow. Orange, red, and yellow silk leaves hung from the ceiling, gently swirling in the air currents.

Smelling cinnamon and cloves, I was momentarily struck with memories of my first Thanksgiving at Dave's house before we were even engaged. That day was filled with so much laughter and fun, and now...

"While I'm getting a few things, I want you to pick out a book to read to Baby. Can you do that?"

Nodding my head yes, I walked over to a circular stand of paperback *GOLDEN Look-Look* books. There wasn't much of a selection, yet I had trouble deciding which book to choose. It was either *Follow the Zookeeper* or *There's No Such Thing as a Dragon*.

"Which one will it be?" Dr. Bobbi said when she returned with a handful of items.

"The Dragdon Boot," I said.

"Would you like this coloring book, too?"

"Yes, pease."

Smiling, she said, "OK, let me pay for everything. Are you up for ice cream?"

I nodded my head yes.

It was a short walk to the small dining area, and as we sat down, I was excited to see real silverware. For a moment, I thought about stealing a knife so I could properly cut my meat when I ate in my room, but I figured I'd get caught and left it on the table.

"Before the ice cream arrives, I need to tell you what happened this morning," Dr. Bobbi said. "There is no easy way, but I know you'll hear about it in the hallways or when you go to dinner tonight, and I wanted you to hear it from me first. Jane— the patient you've been talking to—used the long cord from her telephone to hang herself early this morning. It's a tragic and serious incident. Over the next few days, all phones will be removed from every room. Moving forward, patients will need to ask at the nursing station to check out a phone."

Watching me process the information, Dr. Bobbi took my hand. "I know you admitted to me in one of our sessions that you'd contemplated suicide in the past. All I ask is that you promise me you'll write in your journal or tell me if you ever feel like you need to do something like that. Do you understand?"

Still thinking about Jane, I reluctantly nodded my head. We'd met one afternoon while walking in the hallway. Jane didn't mind that I had Baby, saying she had her own "special friend" in her room. We got into a conversation about Pooh. She said she liked him, too. I offered to lend her my book if she wanted to read it. She gave me a weak smile that day and said thanks. Now, she was gone, and that felt wrong.

Who would miss her? I wondered. But I knew that wasn't the

real question. The true question was, who would miss me if I ever decided it was time to leave this world? My fear was that it would be no one.

On the way back to the ward, Dr. Bobbi informed me that Baby needed to stay in my room. "Some of the other patients don't understand why you have a doll, and it's upsetting to them." When I argued that Baby had to always stay with me, Dr. Bobbi said Baby could go to the sand tray room with me, but that was all. It wasn't perfect, but it was all I could get her to agree to.

At dinner, I speculated about who objected to Baby and when they might leave. Usually, a patient's hospital stay lasted only 21 days, depending on their insurance coverage. Then there was a waiting period before they could return.

The only person I recognized while eating my unappetizing, clumpy spaghetti and meatballs that night was the vet who had PTSD. I thought he must have excellent insurance. Rumor had it he'd been there a long time. Then I wondered about my own insurance. I had no idea how it worked, but Dr. Braun and others involved in the recovered-memory field did. Many years later, I learned through a documentary that hundreds of millions of dollars in healthcare were spent by the end of the satanic panic era in 1992.

When we got back to the room, I said to Baby, "This won't take long. I've put off calling Dave as long as I can. I'll read you our new book when I'm finished."

The adult now appeared to me in a thick, shrouded mist. It was eerie yet captivating to sense the adult blending with the child, who was quickly gaining strength. Each of us seemed to compete in our own way for validation and dominance.

Gathering a corner of the adult me, I picked up the phone and held the long cord in my hand. This was all it took to end a life, I thought, as I dialed and then quickly hung up. Did my number end in 81 or 18? Maybe, I thought, I should wait until tomorrow, but when I heard noises in the hall, I was reminded that my phone could be taken at any minute. I had to do this now.

The phone rang, and when I heard Dave say hello, I breathed a sigh of relief. The 81 number was correct.

"Hi, Dave, it's me."

"Hi," he said in a surprised voice. "I've been wondering when I'd hear from you."

"Sorry, there's been so much going on. I got transferred to a private room, so I don't have a roommate now. I'm in 1314, so if you want to come, you'll have to be let in by staff because the ward is locked."

After a long pause, Dave said, "Yes, I'd like to come see you. Is Saturday good for you?"

I thought no day was a good day for me right now.

But I said, "Sure, weekends are long in this place. Saturday's good."

"OK then," Dave said. "Anything else?"

"No. I'm good for now. I'll see you soon."

# Chapter 17

## *Mommy, I'll Be Good*

There wasn't much to do before Dave arrived. He already knew I had Baby, so I didn't need to hide her. After a breakfast of cold cereal with bananas I'd sliced with my spoon, I took a quick, lukewarm shower. I got out my coloring book and crayons and spent the hours before he arrived coloring and singing the preschool songs from my teaching years.

Vicki was on weekend duty, and luckily, she was the one to lead Dave through the locked door. Sensing I was nervous, she said, "Your door needs to stay open during this visit. OK?" Not trusting my voice, I nodded yes and slid my coloring book toward my pillow.

Dave walked in and sat down on what I called Dr. Braun's chair.

We both stared at each other for a few moments. Time seemed to stand still. We had grown so far apart. I felt my throat tighten as my all-consuming guilt over what I had put us through clung to me like a second skin. I could hardly breathe. Now, what should I talk about? I wondered, as I fought the urge to pick up Baby and put my thumb in my mouth. I don't know this man I've been married to for 13 years. We've never shared our hopes and dreams. The wedding vow of two becoming one never truly happened for us.

"Your doctors let me know you're still being evaluated, but nothing else," he began.

"It's not even two months yet. Dr. Braun said it would be three. They don't tell me anything either."

What I knew, I couldn't reveal. The words "home abuse" and "dissociation" and what was happening in therapy were too strange to think about, let alone share with a man I didn't know.

I never knew what the doctors told Dave, but I do know that my not having close relationships worked in Braun's favor. It was much easier to manipulate me without a spouse or family member objecting or denying the information from my so-called therapy.

Dave shifted in his chair as he took in my sparse surroundings. There wasn't much to see except the thick steel bars covering my room's only window.

"How's Penny?" I asked, really wanting to know if she missed me.

"She's fine. I take her with me on hunting weekends with the guys. She likes being at OZ."

"I'm glad she likes it there."

"You OK?" he asked, looking away from me.

"It's just . . . hard here," I said, my words cut off by "Code white, code white. Dr. Roberts, please report to the nursing station."

Dave flinched, and I shrugged my shoulders. "That's life around here," I said, wondering which patient was in trouble now.

I had nothing more to ask. I didn't know the names of the people he worked with and couldn't remember his friends' names. Leaving the ward to get ice cream wasn't allowed, and I had no desire to show him around a place that still scared me to death. Wiggling, I started to reach for Baby, but I sat on my hands instead.

I saw Dave's eyes flick toward my open door. He also looked like he was struggling with this conversation that wasn't going anywhere. It never had gone anywhere. I had deeper conversations with Penny than I did with Dave. The tension between us was thick. From my bedside view, I noticed Vicki was watching our visit, so on her next pass-by, we made eye contact. She mouthed, "Done?" I gave her a slight nod.

Announcing herself, she knocked on my door. "How's it going, you two?" she asked with a big smile.

Dave glared at her.

"I think it might be best if you kept this visit brief. Sometimes patients find it hard to have visitors."

"Sure, sure," Dave said, quickly getting up from the chair. "Let me know if you need anything."

"I will," I said, smiling weakly. "Thanks for coming."

As I watched him leave, I grabbed Baby in my arms, put my thumb in my mouth, closed my eyes, and let the tears I'd been holding back flow down my face.

Vicki came back after Dave left. She told me she thought Dave was a kind, caring man. "He did ask me questions. And I told him what I was allowed to say, but he's very worried about you."

"Dr. Braun wants me to finish your testing this weekend," Vicki said, watching my body stiffen. A hospital intern had started my promised testing, but Vicki—who was an RN and, I later learned, not qualified to administer psychological testing—was asked to complete it. I suspect Dr. Braun didn't want anyone but his handpicked staff to know who his patients were or what they might say.

Everything during my time at Rush was unconventional at best and criminal at worst. No one was taken to a conference room or office for the standard traditional "talk" therapy. Instead, every one of Dr. Braun's patients had their sessions in their rooms, on their beds. I read, cried, wrote in my journal, underwent hypnosis, talked more about my sand trays, ate, masturbated, and held long conversations with Baby on my bed.

There was nowhere quiet to walk, no fresh air to breathe that could clear my mind of the terrible lies I was beginning to tell in my room. I felt like I was living by the rule I heard at a retreat: "What's said here stays here." I'd hear the leading questions, my half-true answers, and the twisted accusations bouncing around in my mind 24 hours a day.

My only outlets were my journal and the sand tray. In these early months, when I wasn't in a session with Dr. Braun or Dr. Bobbi, I spent much of my alone time sitting on the window's ledge. If I stood on my bed and placed my foot on the headboard, I found I could hoist myself onto the marble ledge, which was broad and sturdy enough for me to sit on.

I loved sitting up there. I felt like I was on the floor of my own private tree house where I was safe and could think but, most of all, be away from the constant noise of the ward. My view from the 13th floor was spectacular. I could see the expressway filled with lights and cars. In the distance, I saw rooftops and trees. Yes, there was still a world beyond my hospital walls. There were clouds and the sun in the morning and, at night, the moon, and if I looked hard enough, I could see a sprinkling of stars. People were driving to work or home to loved ones. Life itself whizzed past me and gave me hope that someday soon, I, too, would be free to come and go as I pleased.

At least, that was my hope. Still, all my therapy seemed to be leading me along an unfamiliar path that, one afternoon, turned especially dark.

Up until that point, no one had mentioned "satanic cult" in any of my sessions. That afternoon I was in the sand tray room, as usual. After an hour, my tray was full of figures that I'd picked at random and the upside-down cross I was using to represent my anger at God and religion. I'd also discovered a set of eight plastic, black-winged creatures that I thought would be fun to use. To me, they resembled the Batman I'd seen on TV in the '60s. I'd just placed my last figure in the tray when Dr. Bobbi walked in. She studied the tray for a moment and then let out a deep sigh. My stomach dropped.

"Would you like to tell me about this tray?" she asked.

With a deep sense I was in some kind of trouble, I shook my head no.

I heard the familiar "Give me your hand, please." I knew my words wouldn't be believed, and even at this early stage of my hospitalization, I had learned the later-debunked finger signals were all that mattered. Still, I gave her my hand.

"Show me a 'yes,'" she said. My "yes" finger lifted. "Very good. Now show me a 'no.'" My middle finger lifted. "Good. Now, everybody listen."

"Is that a satanic animal sacrifice over in the left-hand corner?"

My "yes" finger rose, not because it was true, but because Dr. Bobbi had said my "yes" finger was "very good," and I wanted her praise.

"And over here. Are members having sex with those figures dressed in black robes?"

I watched my "yes" finger rise again. Where was this headed? Were the figures on the shelves manipulated? No matter what I placed in the sand, Dr. Bobbi seemed to find a way to turn the items into something more sinister than I intended.

"Did this take place during the cult ceremony?" Dr. Bobbi asked.

Now inner warning bells were going off, and before my fingers could say "yes," I pulled my hand away from hers and felt the little me arrive.

"Me's knows nofings about satanic ceremonies. Me's don't bemembers doing those fings. Me wikes aminals. Wots!"

"That's because you weren't there, little one. Linda has lost time," Dr. Bobbi said. "She has experienced many terrible things."

"Me's needs to go now, pease," I said as I picked up Baby. I was leaving this room, even if I was supposed to put the sand toys away. This session was too intense for my adult mind to process. I needed to escape everybody and everything, and the only place I could think of was the ledge in my room.

I practically ran back, placing one foot on the headboard and lifting Baby and myself onto the ledge. With Baby secure in my lap, I rested my forehead against the barred window. Linda, think —is there any amount of time you can't account for?

No, I thought, there wasn't. This is crazymaking. How the hell does one lose time? None of the stuff the entire staff suggests I did rings true. I'm sure I don't remember everything in my life, but I think I'd know if I tortured and killed animals in a satanic cult ceremony, wouldn't I? No one in my family is capable of the kind of abuse these doctors say is proven by what I put in the sand.

This internal dialogue and reasoning continued to grow throughout my hospital stay. I knew deep down I had never been abused or involved in a cult, but every staff member seemed to already believe I had done terrible things. They told me that all of Dr. Braun's patients were also recalling some of these same memories. I was no different, they claimed.

I still wanted my diagnosis and treatment plan, so lacking confidence in myself, I gave in to their beliefs and gradually started to believe maybe they were right, and I had simply blocked my cult memories from my mind. Like with my sexual acting out, the sand tray became my obsessive need to tell their stories, which were not true. Repeatedly, I'd tell an untrue story, adding details I uncovered during my so-called recovered-memory therapy sessions.

I'd had fun building my first few trays. I got attention and felt special. I had a crush on Dr. Bobbi, but after this tray, I suspected that she and Dr. Braun were searching for evidence about something else. I was panicked over what I'd just heard in the sand room. I needed to deny I belonged to a satanic cult, and I guessed that shouting "No, it's not true" wasn't going to make any difference, but I did it anyway. It felt good to be defiant and speak my truth, but my defiance came with a price.

Out of nowhere, a passing aide entered my room. "Can you please come down from there?" I didn't answer or try to come down. I'd been seen on this ledge dozens of times. So why should

I come down today? I wasn't a danger to myself or anyone else. No, I needed to stay here until I understood what was happening to me.

Within a few minutes, I heard Kate's voice. "Linda, you need to come down from that ledge right now."

Breathing hard and wanting to say, Go to hell! I shook my head no, no, no.

"Then I'm afraid you'll have to be taken to QR."

I didn't have time to think about what that meant as four orderlies rushed into my room and roughly pulled me off the ledge. In my already frantic mind, their hands became a memory of my mother's, as she roughly yanked my stiff, scared body off the toilet when I refused to pee on demand. When I heard Baby fall to the floor, I screamed, "NO! I'll be good, I'll be good, Mommy, please, I'll be good, I'll be gooood! No don't take me away."

They carried me down a long hallway. I felt like a captured animal as Dr. Bobbi stood silently by the open Quiet Room door, watching as they placed my body onto a low bed. Expertly, the aides buckled my arms and legs into leather straps. With tears in her eyes, Dr. Bobbi held my hand as a nurse entered and injected something into the vein of my left arm. Soon, the room blurred as I felt my terrified body begin to fade into nothingness.

# Chapter 18

## *Bad News*

On the morning of November 21, 1985, Dr. Bobbi and Dr. Braun entered my room. Their faces looked solemn, which felt unusual. Dr. Bobbi always smiled when she came into my room. A cream-colored rotary phone with its long, twisted cord wrapped around it was in her hands. I remembered using that same kind of phone before they were taken out of our rooms and wondered why it was being brought to me now. Dr. Braun stayed silent as Dr. Bobbi plugged it in and placed it on my tray table. She then took both of my hands in hers and said, "Your mother will be calling you in a few minutes."

"Why," I asked in a little voice.

"We need a big person here right now," Dr. Bobbi said as the phone rang.

I picked up the receiver. "Hello?"

The voice was quivering but still recognizable. "Daddy died this morning. He's gone, he's gone."

I tried to speak, but words failed me. I felt as if I were caught between the living and the dead. Nothing, including myself, felt real. Mom's wrong, I thought. She misunderstood someone's conversation. I'd just seen my dad. He was worried about me, and a week earlier, he had managed to slip through the locked doors of my ward. He hadn't mentioned being sick, but Mom sounded way too upset. It had to be true. What would happen to her now that Dad was gone?

I guess I'd been silent too long because Dr. Bobbi took the receiver from my hand and said to Dr. Braun, "She's dissociated," and then spoke into the receiver. "Hi Mrs. um . . . Linda is having difficulty with this information right now. I'm Dr. Sachs, one of her doctors. Can she call you back soon?"

Turning to me, Dr. Bobbi said, "When you calm down a bit, you can call your mom back, OK? In the meantime, open your mouth and let me put a Xanax under your tongue. It gets into your system faster that way."

This was the first time I took Xanax sublingually. I remember it tasting like SweeTARTS, which reminded me of stopping at the candy store on the way home from school. I preferred other candies, but the SweeTARTS had vibrant colors and lasted longer. Their sweet and sour flavor was unique, just like the Xanax now dissolving into bitter grit under my tongue.

As the pill dissolved, I heard both doctors quietly discussing whether I should be allowed to leave the ward for the wake and funeral. I heard Dr. Braun say, "If she leaves, she could be abducted and taken back to the cult. We can't let that happen."

"I agree," Dr. Bobbi said, "Besides, she's way too fragile, but she does need to be given a choice."

Did I hear that wrong? Dissociated? Yes, I was in shock, but what are they talking about? I wondered. My doctors should be trying to help me cope with a major loss, instead they're talking to each other like I'm not here and saying . . . what?

I didn't understand. I would be at a funeral home with Dave and relatives. When would there be a chance for someone to abduct me? This made no sense even to my confused mind.

Not realizing I had heard them talking, Dr. Bobbi sat beside me on my bed.

"Hey, cutie, this is tough stuff. I'm so sorry. Both Dr. Braun and I think you shouldn't leave the ward right now. What do you think?"

I said nothing because I didn't know what to think. I didn't trust myself to leave the ward. I felt so young, so out of touch with reality, so scared to be with Dave again. Everywhere I looked, there was death—death of the self I knew, as well as the death that supposedly occurred in some vague cult. No, a funeral home was not where I wanted to be. Going to the hospital gift shop had been hard enough. I couldn't see myself standing in a line saying, "So nice of you to come" in a grown-up voice.

When I started to feel disconnected from my body, I knew the Xanax was working, so I quickly asked, "Can I call my mom now?"

"Sure," Dr. Bobbi said.

I struggled to recall the correct number and felt relief when I heard crying. I recognized that cry as one of a wounded animal. I'd heard it many times as a child. "Hi Mom, it's me. Tell me what happened."

"I don't know," she kept saying. "Daddy died in the hospital, but I don't know what he died from or where the funeral or burial will be. Your brothers are taking care of that. What am I going to do now?"

I couldn't help her. I could barely help myself, but still trying to be the good girl, I asked her if she wanted me to come home.

"No, no," she said, "you stay where you're at. You need to get well. I've got to go." And just like that, she hung up.

There was instant relief because I knew even if Mom had said "yes, you need to come home," I would have found an excuse not to go.

And that's when the guilt hit me. I was wimping out. Wasn't being with my mom and family at a time like this expected? I knew very well it was my responsibility as the oldest child and only daughter to be there to support them. Yet I knew deep in my gut that going home wouldn't be the smart choice.

Still holding the receiver, I turned to Dr. Bobbi and said, "She told me not to come."

"That's good. Because we weren't going to let you go anyway."

Staff checked on me often. I was aware every eye was on me. Each med cup held another Xanax, making it impossible to think clearly. I wanted to write about how I felt but couldn't hold my pen as the words kept slipping off the page. Tears and anger over what was happening were all trapped inside. My eyes kept closing. The only option was to give in to the drug and fall into a Xanax-induced sleep.

I was in between worlds when Dr. Bobbi came into my room for her last evening check. "I've heard that you've not eaten all day. I brought you some soup."

"Me no wants it."

"Ah, little one, that's not what the doctor ordered," she said. "Now open wide. You need something in your tummy."

Giggling, I accepted the first spoonful of near-warm chicken soup.

"I've talked with your husband and told him you wouldn't be attending your father's services," Dr. Bobbi said after I finished the last of the small cup. "Dave said he was disappointed, but he understood. And tonight, you'll be sleeping in the hallway by the nursing station."

"Why? Me no wants to sleep there."

"We need to make sure that you're safe tonight."

"No, no, no, no, no."

"You don't want another trip to the quiet room, do you?"

Pulling in my breath, I quietly said, "No, me's be good."

"Good," she said, pushing my hair back. "Give me a hug and get Baby ready for bed. I'll see you first thing in the morning."

At 9 p.m., Vicki brought in another pill. "No more," I said.

"Sorry, Dr. Braun's orders. This one will help you sleep."

I considered spitting out the drug as Vicki bent down and

released the brakes from the wheels on my bed, but QR was not a place I wanted to revisit.

"Here she is," a nurse said in a jovial voice when we arrived. "Our guest for the night. Let's get you parked where we can keep an eye on you."

Over the next few days, I wondered if my calls were being monitored because I heard nothing more about my dad's death or arrangements. I thought for sure one of my brothers would get in touch. But everything was silent, and I was left to grieve alone.

Even Dr. Bobbi didn't ask a ton of questions when a man in a coffin appeared in my sand tray. My fingers agreed the man was my dad, not some cult victim, and she let it go.

# Chapter 19

---

## *Broken Promises*

Because of my father's death, Dr. Braun insisted I needed supervision. Each night after 9 p.m. meds, my bed was rolled down the hall to the nursing station. Sometimes I was in it. Other times, I'd stagger down the corridor, sedated with a strong sleep medication called Halcion, trying to hide the feeling that I was on display for everyone to see.

A few spindly plastic Christmas wreaths and colored lights appeared at the nursing station and dining area over the next few weeks. Paper candy canes were placed on our doors. Baby and I ripped ours down on the first day, which made Dr. Braun think I knew more about the upcoming holidays than I did. He understood there were special cult ceremonies during this time. When he asked if I knew what took place during them, I shook my head no. His response was, "Does anyone inside know?"

"Anyone inside" was becoming clearer, but I still wasn't sure what it all meant. With no leading questions to guide me and unsure how to respond, I stayed silent. Dr. Braun didn't press for more because he knew what was coming next.

Part of me knew I wouldn't be going home before Christmas. Still, I wasn't ready for what Dr. Bobbi had to say when she entered my room early Friday afternoon on December 20. I had just finished tying green and white ribbons in Baby's pigtails when she appeared and sat close to me on my bed.

Taking my hand, she said, "Dr. Braun and I met with your team.

She sighed. And I knew something big was coming.

"All signs suggest that you have taken part in satanic ritual cult activities. Your use of red stones, animals, coffins, babies, and upside-down crosses in your trays are all part of the many satanic ceremonies Buddy and I are hearing about."

"No, no, no. Not true."

"Every day, your trays provide more evidence that you have personally sacrificed animals and participated in blood rituals. I also believe you understand what it's like to be placed in a coffin and have had numerous ritual sexual encounters. It's clear to all of us from your long periods of silence, strange behaviors, and results from your psychological tests that you have endured severe abuse at home as well."

I was speechless.

She continued, "You also dissociate, and it is my belief you are poly-fragmented. You're like a glass vase that's fallen to the floor and shattered into thousands of pieces. You have little to nothing that is whole.

"Do you understand? You're a very sick lady, Linda, and you're not going anywhere anytime soon. Try two to three years, for starters. For starters."

I didn't understand. Shock ran through me as my hands rose in the air. "But it's not true," I cried. "I want to go home. None of this is true. I made it all up. I did. Really. It's all lies."

I thought this hospitalization would make me better. But it didn't. I no longer recognized who I was or what I believed. It felt as if I had walked through an open door into a land where everything I knew was gone.

"Why would you make up lies like this?" Dr. Bobbi asked.

Why had I?

"I put those things in the sand," I said, "because, because, I thought, that's what you and Dr. Braun wanted to see? Me's has a good imagination."

"If that's what you need to believe, for now, that's OK," she said, taking me in her arms and letting me cry. "What's happened to you is too painful for you to remember and take in all at once. So, it's OK if your mind needs to take a break, because there is a whole lot more yet to come."

She then sang "Hush Little Baby," and rocked me for a long time. Vicki must have come in because I became aware of the taste of SweeTARTS and soon I could feel my tense body relax.

"I know this is hard for you to understand," Dr. Bobbi said, "but you're not safe to go home right now. Here's Baby. Take a little nap. I'll stop in before I leave for the night." And, planting a kiss on my forehead, she left my room.

I woke up to a plate of coagulated food on my tray table. The sight of it made my stomach turn. With unsteady, rubbery legs, I made my way to the sink. Running cold water over a faded, thin white washcloth, I pressed it to my snot-smeared face and swollen eyes.

I sat back on my bed, picked up Baby, and looked around in disbelief. This hospital and postage-sized room were now my home for the foreseeable future. I'd been betrayed by the mental health system. I was promised a diagnosis and treatment plan, but what I got was a convoluted diagnosis from a man who believed there was growing evidence that satanists had been ritually abusing children for a long time. He and Dr. Bobbi were confident that, with time, they could help me recover my forgotten and repressed memories. And then, and only then, could I heal.

Dr. Bobbi never commented on my sexual experiences. Nor did she ever question my fingers. Instead, what I wrote in my journal was used to strengthen my involvement in the cult. I now believe that Braun and Bobbi lacked any background or understanding of unstable family dynamics, sexual compulsions, or intimacy issues. It wasn't within their mindset or expertise, so rather than abandon their fame and insurance money and refer me to another psychiatrist, they turned my behavior into something dark, perverse, and false.

Nothing made sense that day. I didn't know what to do or where to turn. I knew I wouldn't even last a day in the real world now. I couldn't leave and I couldn't go home.

Dr. Bobbi arrived with Vicki just as my bed was being pushed into the hall again. "I brought you a Halcion," Vicki said. I wanted to ask, are you kidding? I already feel like rubber. But all I could do was shake my head no.

"No meds?" Dr. Bobbi asked.

"Not that one," I answered. "You know none of this stuff is true, don't you?"

"It is true, Linda, and the sooner you recognize it, the better off you'll be. Now give me a hug. I'll see you in the morning."

Crap, I wondered after she left, why can't I be mad at her? She's completely turned my whole life upside down. I had refused the Halcion, but as I was pulling the covers over myself, I was handed my med cup. Maybe Halcion wasn't there, but something was, because the next thing I knew, I was glancing at the oversized clock hanging over the nursing station.

It was now 6 a.m. on Sunday, December 22. "Well, Baby, in 18 minutes, I'll be 40. Never in a million years did I ever think I'd be starting this new decade of my life holding a doll and looking forward to a day of endless nothingness."

When my bed was returned to my room, I showered and, on a whim while getting dressed, decided to remove my wedding ring. Even if it was just in my mind, I wanted to start my 40th year unmarried. It felt good until a nurse popped her head into my room.

"Your husband is on the line. Do you want to talk to him?" For a moment, I panicked and felt guilty. Did he know I'd taken off my ring? No, that was silly. Still, I didn't want to talk to him. I didn't want to tell him I wasn't coming home. Saying it out loud made it real, and I wasn't ready for that.

"No," I said. "Tell him I'm in therapy with my nurse." She

did, but an hour later he called back. Gathering what little reserves I had, I went to the nurses' station and took the call.

"Hey," he said, in a cheerful voice. "Happy birthday and Merry Christmas."

"Thanks," I said, "tell everyone Merry Christmas from me too. I still don't have a phone, and . . ."

"I know," he said. "Are you coming home soon? I still don't know anything."

"Um, I'm not sure. Look, Dave, I've got to go. Someone wants to use this phone. Give Penny a kiss from me. I'll be in touch soon."

Some things never change, I thought as I hung up the phone. Even in the hospital Happy Birthday Merry Christmas are all run together. He did remember my birthday, though. He does care. Could I go back home and start over? I pulled my journal out of the vanity drawer and spent the day writing pros and cons that, in the end, didn't matter. I wasn't going anywhere.

The little one, now called "the presenting personality," was out most of every day. I sucked my thumb and avoided direct eye contact with anyone. I could feel the real world fading away.

I didn't refuse the Halcion that night. I couldn't wait to leave this world of confusion behind.

Both doctors entered my room with presents early the next afternoon. "Happy birthday," they both said. The Linda who had checked into Rush was gone, leaving a child and a vacant-eyed adult to open a gift from Dr. Braun. He had signed his name and "Best Wishes" in a picture book called *William's Doll*. The adult me undid the wrapping, while the child me said the proper thank you.

Dr. Bobbi's present was a card with a cat curled up by a fireplace and a snow-white Gund teddy bear named Snuggles, who immediately took her place next to Baby.

Later, Dr. Braun informed me that a new unit would open in early January. "I'm very excited about this unit," he said. "We now have trained staff and invaluable diagnostic tools. The old critical care floor moved to the main building, so we will have our own Dissociative Disorder Unit. This will not be a ward, but an entire unit specifically for multiple personality and satanic ritual abuse patients."

Years later, I learned that satanic ritual abuse stories first appeared in the early 1980s, when allegations of ritualized child sexual abuse were made against numerous preschool and daycare workers across the United States. Children were cross-examined with leading questions, which resulted in staff being charged with sexual abuse, satanism, and animal sacrifice. By the end, it had become the longest and most costly series of criminal trials in American history. They left hundreds of children emotionally damaged and also destroyed many staff members' careers. Those events triggered what some called a moral panic, or satanic panic. In 1987, Geraldo Rivera aired a national television special about these alleged secret cults. Soon, belief spread through churches that asked their congregations, "Do you know where your children are?" Religious groups also warned parents that satanic messages were hidden in records—messages that could be heard if some songs were played backward.

"And you, along with the other people Dr. Braun and I work with, will be our first patients," Dr. Bobbi added. "We will have our own playroom and a sand tray room. I have a friend who is busy buying toys now.

"To keep you safe," Dr. Braun said as he left, "you will be sleeping by the nursing station until after New Year's. Have a good day."

That night, Baby and I fell asleep under the bright lights to the song "O Holy Night." Shit, I thought, waiting for the Halcion to ease the brutal, gut-wrenching pain. It feels more like "O Lonely Night." Three more years, I thought, with tears surfacing again. Dear God, this is way more than I ever bargained for. So please, I just want to die. I really do. And this time, I mean it.

# Chapter 20

## *Who's Here?*

"Welcome to the new unit," Kate said. "You're the first patient to arrive. The rest of Dr. Braun's patients are on their way. You'll be in room 247. My note says you'll have a new roommate on Monday. Which bed would you like?"

"I don't want a roommate."

"There are no private rooms in this unit. You, like all the rest, are going to have to share this space."

"Then I'll take the one by the window," I said, as I sat Baby on the bed.

I knew it was imaginary, but I needed to have control over something, even if it was only opening and closing the drapes at my discretion. I'd already lost so much independence.

My new room didn't have a ledge or a view of the expressway, which made me sad. Where could I find a sense of life outside?

When I finished putting away my few belongings, I allowed myself to explore my new surroundings. This unit was T-shaped, with the nursing station situated in the center. I counted ten double rooms. There was the standard lounge/TV room, art room, playroom, and the promised sand tray room.

I shivered as I passed two quiet rooms. Looking closer, I saw they were numbered QR 1 and QR 2. I guessed that one room had a bed with leather straps, and the purpose of the other would be revealed to me soon enough.

I noticed a few women I'd seen on Thirteen while looking into other rooms. I had wondered who the rest of Dr. Braun's patients were. There would be many over the years. In the end, I would share a room with fifty-five different women. Margo from Pennsylvania was one of them. She was friendly enough, and we sometimes talked during her brief stay. When she left the ward, she said her insurance wouldn't cover another hospital stay. I never saw her again. This became the usual pattern of my revolving-door roommates.

One of the patients who was among the first to sue Braun was also my roommate for a short time. We had the same insurance, so she, like me, was kept as long as possible.

Insurance played a major role in determining how long a patient could stay in the unit. Some could only stay up to three weeks and then couldn't return for at least sixty days. Others, like Margo, were denied readmission. Different states had different policies that would either deny or limit mental health hospitalizations. Money was always a key factor in every case. No insurance coverage meant no return to a hospital which, in my opinion, was a gain for the patient. Even if the therapist believed their patient was in a cult and was treating her for that, at least she was in her own environment and had a small chance of seeing that what she was being led to believe was false.

Years later, I would wonder why no men had been admitted to Dr. Braun's unit. During my research, I found that other units in various states were also mostly women. Yet most of us were being manipulated mainly by male psychiatrists. Where did these misinformed doctors think our sacrificial babies came from? Who did I and all these women share orgies with? Who raped us? Why weren't there any men in therapy being questioned about their role in all this?

I was tired of being asked, "Who's here?" One Saturday afternoon, I took my last large piece of white drawing paper and a sharp pencil to the playroom. I figured that if everyone on staff wanted to know who's here, then I'd make up names and put them on this paper. Maybe then the staff would just shut up.

At first, like in the sand, I had fun. I named the angry part of me Margaret and my compulsive, sexual self, Valerie. Then, the naming turned dark, as I also gave names to the "alters" Drs. Bobbi and Braun said had killed animals, participated in those unimaginable blood sacrifices, and had sex while doing things that made my stomach turn. These weren't "personality parts" like my anger and sexual self, that Braun and Bobbi now called alters. These darker alters supposedly held my secrets.

For me, it didn't matter that I was making up these pretend alters. All that was important was that I had names, so when the "Who's here?" question was asked, I had answers.

The most difficult part to name was the child who seemed to be gaining more strength. She felt as real to me as someone with skin. Yet, at the same time, she felt like an imaginary friend I compared to Becky Thatcher in *Tom Sawyer*. Lacking something more creative, I named her Becky. I saw Becky as the innocent part of me that was capable of love. I thought she held my happiness. Only together could we survive.

We survived, but looking back, creating her was the most life-changing thing I was ever emotionally forced to do. I did not have multiple personalities when I arrived at the ward. I came to the hospital with compulsions, not personalities. I had many toddler-like behaviors, but even though fragile, I was still whole.

In my desperate search for help, I could only stay whole for so long, and I believe Braun knew that. Now I existed in an environment where, no matter what I said, I wasn't believed. I had been denied saying my final goodbyes to my dad and had been made to sleep in the hall, pumped full of drugs that made me feel like I was an alien. The worst part, though, was that I knew the promise of a diagnosis and treatment plan had been broken. I had lost all hope of understanding why I had compulsions and couldn't love my husband. This was too much for my severely confused mind to handle.

So, while I sensed Becky and all the other parts of me, or "alters," weren't real, I also felt that if I didn't play Braun's game, I would completely lose my mind. To keep any sense of myself, I had created alters that, in Bobbi's and Braun's minds, participated in cult activities. Then I had the presence of mind to give my heart and soul to the sane and innocent part of myself I named Becky, who, in her own sweet and creative ways, kept my core and survival instincts intact.

This did play on my psyche, though. I was no longer the same person who had gotten off the elevator on that warm September afternoon. What would be the result of this made-up stuff, and who would I be if I ever managed to get out of this insane place that was now my home?

Years after I was discharged from the hospital and living on my own, I joined a Unitarian church. I became friends with the pastor and told her about my hospitalization and Dr. Braun. She was quiet for a moment, then told me she had taken hypnosis classes, and Dr. Braun was a participant in some of them. She clearly remembered Braun boasting that through hypnosis and asking the right questions, he could get his patients to admit to having other personalities.

Braun was skilled at asking questions with double meanings. In one or two hypnosis sessions at most, most patients would admit to having alters. These alters then supposedly committed crimes that happened without our knowledge. From that point on, he would distort everything we said into his diagnosis. And when the sessions ended and you were alone, you would break down in tears because you had no idea what had just happened to you.

He did get me to admit I had parts/alters/personalities inside and, after that, it was easy to lead me to believe I was also a victim of ritual abuse. Therapy never changed. I became a long-term patient. All they needed to do was keep me sick enough to continue collecting my insurance money. So, five days a week, I received double talk, coercion, sand trays, and finger signals. Period.

Through leading questions, I was given all the "right tools" to create Becky, a "personality part." My vulnerability was encouraged and enhanced through drugs, positive reinforcement, and my compulsive need to please Dr. Bobbi.

Becky was rewarded with hugs, many toys, and special care as trauma was heaped on trauma. During my fourth year, I learned about a way to integrate my "cult alters," but no one ever told me how to undo the child I had created to help keep me sane.

When I left the hospital, the nonsense-made-up cult alters disappeared. Becky, however, did not. By then, the two of us were one.

Depending on the circumstances, studies say it takes anywhere from eighteen to 254 days for a new behavior to become automatic. I had 1,460 days to perfect Becky's speech, gait, and her likes and dislikes. She was now her own independent self. We blended like we were both born in the same pea pod and seamlessly switched back and forth, operating as a team.

My room was always the first stop Dr. Bobbi made when she arrived on the unit. She was wearing my favorite multicolored blouse and black skirt and within seconds she heard, "Hi, me's has a name."

"You do. What is it?"

"My name's Becky."

"Where did you get the name?"

"Winda gaved it to me."

"See," Becky said, pulling out the charts I made. "It has wots of names on it."

Dr. Bobbi took the paper and studied it for a long time.

"Where did this come from, Linda?"

"From inside," I quietly said. "You and Dr. Braun wanted names of who's here, so here they are."

I'm not sure what she thought that day, but unlike me, I know she never questioned the validity of the names on the paper. I wondered if she knew I had made them up, but she was unwilling to challenge anything so I could stay longer. Then I thought, no one could be that unethical.

Vicki was the only person who questioned the sudden explosion of names, but like the rest of the staff, it didn't take long for Becky, Margaret, and Valerie to become as familiar as if they had been there since day one.

The first conference of the International Society for the Study of Multiple Personality and Dissociation was held in 1983. It was widely attended by therapists interested in dissociation and multiplicity. Dr. Braun became president of this association in 1984 and continued to promote his theory that satanic cults were everywhere. When I came under his care in 1985, he was well on his way to gaining notoriety. Unfortunately, through this conference alone, false information and stories spread around the world faster than lightning.

It was after one of these conferences during my second year that another falsehood was planted.

"Many therapists at the conference Buddy and I attended over the weekend reported their clients have gotten pregnant during satanic gatherings," Dr. Bobbi said, as she picked up my hand. "I know you've denied being pregnant, but I think it's time you faced it. You know I'm right. It's been in your sand trays all along. You've been pregnant, probably, many times."

"No," I protested. "I would know if I was ever pregnant."

"That's not true," Bobbi said, as if she was telling me some everyday thing. "You may not remember, but some alter does. Think about that, write if you have to. I'll see you first thing in the morning and we'll talk more."

This was beyond me. There was no way in hell I was ever pregnant. This was insane.

I did write, but all it did was increase my anxiety and intensify my urge for a sexual outlet. This time, I wanted to make an obscene phone call. All phones had been moved back to our rooms, now connected to short cords that we couldn't hang ourselves with. I'd considered this before, but at home, I always managed to distract myself with Dave's magazines and avoid doing it.

The thought was unrelenting. Even with Xanax and an early Halcion, every crude word echoed in my mind. My desires paralleled my car-ride days. I was beyond caring about the consequences.

I closed the door and removed my clothes. Then, sitting on the bed, I let my fingers travel to the place of pleasure, picked up the phone, and randomly dialed.

"Hello," a soft-spoken female voice answered.

"Ah," I said, "I want to lick your pussy and make you . . ."

"Oh, you poor dear," I heard. "I feel so sorry for you. How can I help?"

The spell was broken. Clarity and a flood of tears came as I slammed down the phone.

How can you help? I thought. Tell me what's wrong with me. Help me understand that sex is normal. Hold me, tell me that you want and need me. Tell me that what I feel can be fixed and get me the HELL out of here before I completely lose my mind. Help me not to want to end this godforsaken, goddamned life I'm living.

The inner pain was so overwhelming I was sure my heart would burst at any moment. I so, so, so wanted to die.

"Please, please, somebody help," I muttered as I dressed in PJs and my brown sweater. Thankfully, the Halcion took hold and soon I drifted off to the land of wild drug dreams.

I have no idea who I spoke with that night. All I know is that call did more for me than any psychiatrist ever could. Instead of reacting with judgment and screaming, "You pervert, what the hell is wrong with you," that unknown woman showed me compassion. She offered help—help that was not coming from "my expert team."

I never made another obscene phone call. I did other sexual things that embarrassed me. But that night, I was truly given a gift. It ended one of my many compulsions.

# Chapter 21

## *Desperation Sets In*

My suicidal feelings intensified. I didn't have any actual memories of cult activities, but I did remember the decision I made not to have children. So, yes, if I had found myself pregnant, it would have been a very big deal for me and something I would definitely remember.

Staff often checked on me to see if I was OK and kept my door wide open. Outwardly, I appeared like my usual, regressed self. But inside, I was a mess and spent my time writing journal entries. Some I kept, some I tore apart in anger, but the one I left open for Bobbi to read was the one that revealed what was really going on inside.

*Me. They. I wants to die now!*

*DIE.*

*We had no babies.*

*We never had no babies!!!*

*Me's needs to doe home now pease."*

"Who wrote these?" Bobbi asked.

I shrugged my shoulders. "Me, I guess."

It didn't matter what language or form my words were in, all I knew was the only way out of my pain and confusion was to die.

"Do you have a plan?"

No, I thought. I don't. I'd tested the flimsy shower rod and checked every inch of my room for a possible place to hang or strangle myself. I could make a rope out of my bed sheets, but then what? All I had was one lonely pill I'd managed not to swallow, but that wasn't enough to kill me.

"No, I don't have a plan."

Even so, I was immediately placed on suicide watch. For the next forty-eight hours, I sat within arm's reach of a nurse or aide and was accompanied to the bathroom when needed. All doors were kept open, and when asked, I had to verbally confirm I was OK.

I let out a slow breath and grabbed my brown sweater, Baby, *Winnie the Pooh*, journal, and pen. I didn't want to talk, so I mindlessly turned pages in Pooh while wishing a hole would open and I could drop out of sight.

At the start of the watch, I had many arguments about my meds. The small white cup held a purple Xanax and another new pill. No one told me what it was. I swallowed both, wondering how these would make me feel better.

As a compromise, my team said I could choose the color of my Xanax. Peach was 0.5 mg, purple was 1 mg. The white one, 2 mg, was reserved for major meltdowns or emotionally overwhelming sessions. However, this compromise didn't last long. I would often ask for peach but get purple instead. I realized then that my choice had been taken away, and I was just glad the pill was purple and not white.

Dr. Braun also increased my Inderal dosage. I would eventually learn that Inderal was mainly used as a heart medication and had not been approved by the Food and Drug Administration for treating multiple personality disorders. However, this controversial drug was standard for all of Dr. Braun's patients. He believed that Inderal helped slow down the switching of personalities.

By the end of my four years at the hospital, I was taking 1,040 mg of Inderal daily, which is ten times higher than the maximum dose typically given to heart patients. Now, I have heart issues. I've asked my doctors if the Inderal could be linked to that. They all say no, but I still wonder.

Eating was tough since I was only given a plastic spoon. I couldn't eat chicken and mashed potatoes with just a spoon, so I, as Becky, started eating all my meals with my fingers. Staff quickly decided it would be better for me to eat in my room under supervision instead of the dining room.

At the end of my forty-eight hours, I'd had enough. I still wanted to die, but I couldn't stand being attached to a nurse or aide constantly. I also couldn't come up with a plan to kill myself, so when asked if I thought I was OK to come off the hard watch, I crossed my fingers and said, "yes."

Even on the best days, my mind kept searching for a way to end it all. At one point, I began to swipe the plastic bags that held the fresh linens. Even though I was sure I'd hidden them well under Baby's clothes, they were discovered during a room search, and yet another plan was foiled.

The most serious threat arose when I decided to improve myself and recover on my own. I overheard a conversation one day in the dining room about a form called an "AMA," or a request for discharge "Against Medical Advice." It seemed that since I was self-admitted, I could refuse "recommended treatment."

My plan wasn't to present as Becky or anyone else. I wanted to convince the staff that I had made everything up, and then they would let me go. However, this wasn't logical thinking, since I still had no money and nowhere to go. I had pushed Dave too far and didn't think he would take me back with open arms. But with my flawed reasoning, I was convinced it would work.

I still changed Baby into PJs every night and slipped into toddler language on occasion, but, over the next few days, I managed to function like the adult I sort of remembered being. During the day, I dressed with more care, curled my hair, and didn't play with any of the toys in my room. At night, I politely refused my Halcion.

It took great concentration to hold it together, but instead of creating a tray full of supposed cult activities, I filled it with trees, fake flowers, and blue stones to resemble a lake. I then wrote in my journal how sorry I was for lying about everything. The staff didn't question my behavior, yet I felt every eye watching me wherever I went.

Around the fourth day, Kate stopped by my room to ask if I was going to the sand room that day. I couldn't wait any longer. I was obsessed with leaving the hospital.

"No," I said, "not today, but I would like an AMA form, please."

"That will need to be discussed with Dr. Braun and your team," she said. "I'll check back with you later."

Later, both Bobbi and Braun came to my room.

"So, I hear you want to leave," Dr. Braun said.

"Yes, please," I said in my best adult voice.

"Do you know what AMA means?"

"Yes, it means, um, to leave without . . . shit," I was beginning to panic.

"You do have the right to leave, but with your current state of mind, you wouldn't last ten minutes outside," Dr. Braun continued in his usual patronizing tone. "You have nowhere to go. And if you try to leave, we'll inform the police that your chart shows you're a danger to yourself and others."

The mention of police was all it took for me to completely break down. My heart pounded as tears gathered in my eyes. In the end, my rights didn't matter. In an instant, the adult disappeared. With pain as intense as being punched in the stomach, I lost all hope of ever leaving the hospital. I was powerless, caught in a world of induced sedation and unbearable lies. I couldn't leave, and I couldn't die. But I could try.

That suicide watch lasted a week. Becky took over, but even her bright demeanor seemed dulled. Once again, I was taken to my room at mealtime. I needed a change of clothes after nearly every meal. My thumb went back to my mouth, and Baby never left my side.

Dr. Bobbi spent her time either holding me or making popping sounds with her finger in her cheek as she walked past me in the hallway. Nothing changed until one afternoon when she said, "Staff has agreed when the time is right, you can ask for a divorce."

I kept asking after every visit with Dave if I could tell him I wanted out of the marriage. The answer was always the same: it's protocol that no major changes should happen in a patient's life while in the hospital.

I thought that was a silly rule, but even staff agreed that Dave's infrequent visits were hard to watch. He came every few months to bring me personal supplies or more clothes, but after the "Hi, how are you," we mostly just looked at each other.

Now, finally, my foggy mind thought, I won't be married if and when I get out of here. I couldn't think beyond that. The thought of starting over on my own gave me a tiny seed of hope and helped me get through the next days, weeks, and months.

I was extremely anxious that Saturday when I knew I would tell Dave I wanted a divorce. Because of my suicide watches, it had been over three months since I last saw him. I'll be 42 in December, and I hadn't seen anyone else from my outside life in two years. Every day, I only saw familiar hospital staff and the faces of new patients who came and went like a toy train on a circular track.

It's hard to fully explain my feelings, but when Vicki and Dave walked in, I felt like I was caught up in a hazy dream.

Who are you, I wondered. His face looked familiar, but it bore lines I didn't recognize. Silver glints shimmered in his hair. My memory then flashed a brief image of him, so young, in the break room asking me out for the first time. All of this could have been so different, I thought, if only I hadn't taken my engagement ring back.

Reality snapped back. "How was the drive in?"

"Fine, fine," he said, looking wide-eyed at all my toys and books.

"Good," I said, "and Penny?"

"She's good, too."

A heavy silence filled the room as I cleared my throat. "There's no easy way to say this, but for both of our sakes, I want a divorce. I see no end to this hospitalization, and I've put us through enough. I can't be married anymore."

I'm unsure whether it's what I wanted to see or if he genuinely seemed relieved by my announcement. He asked if I was sure.

"Yes," I said, as we both looked at my finger, still without the diamond that had long lost its sparkle. "I'm sure."

It was done. It was over. He'd left my room like a mirage dissolving when the light changes. I was about to be free from being a married woman. Yet at that moment, I felt so empty, so lost, so alone, scared I'd become a bag lady or a permanent ward of the state. I couldn't cry. I wouldn't cry. If I didn't tuck every goddamned thought and feeling back inside, I feared I would have that psychotic break I was so worried about. My mind felt tissue-paper thin. I could splinter in a heartbeat.

Vicki found me on the bed with Baby, successfully back in a world of no feeling.

"Hey," she said, "do you need a Xanax?"

I shook my head no. I was already numb.

"But I will take a Halcion before bed, please."

"Sure."

"Dave said he'd do what needs to be done and will be in touch by phone when he has more information."

"On second thought, I think I'd like that Xanax." I wanted to say make it five, but instead said, "and make it a white one, please."

# Chapter 22

## *Green Dots*

Dave reached out again during my third year at Rush. Our house was being put on the market. Could I come pick out what I wanted to keep?

I didn't expect this. It wouldn't be easy to see where my old life had been, but I wanted the family photos and anything else that could help me remember where I came from. On the day we arranged to meet, I was back on suicide watch. The hospital sent Vicki with me.

"Xanax?" she asked.

"I'll take peach, please."

My body had adjusted to the Xanax and taking it now was like taking baby aspirin. It only dulled the edges of my feelings. Still, the wiggly, Jell-O-like sensation filled every inch of my stomach.

Dave picked us up in my Honda Civic—the car I had completely forgotten I owned. I hadn't been on a highway since I'd left home, so I was sure Dave was driving a hundred miles an hour. The scenery blurred. My ears rang and my heart raced.

"Breathe," I heard Vicki say. "If you breathe, you'll feel better."

Gradually, the world stopped spinning, allowing me to take in the stores, children, billboards—and life.

At first, I didn't know where I was when we pulled up to a white garage. But then, like a magician pulling back a curtain, everything clicked into stunning clarity. I was home.

I had a few unsteady moments as I pulled myself out of the back seat. OK, Linda, I said to myself as we all walked toward the front door and stepped into the foyer. You can do this.

"I thought it would be easier for you to put these green dots on what you'd like to keep," Dave said in a slow, calm voice. "I'll box up everything for you." He faltered, looking at Vicki.

"She's having a tough time," Vicki said.

My eyes swiveled back and forth. I felt like a child being discussed between her parents—as if I weren't there.

Somehow, I found my voice. "I'd like to take my children's books with me."

Most days, I struggled to tell reality from fantasy. But this, I knew, was real. This had once been my home—my belongings. But now it wasn't. Not anymore. Someone—probably Dave's mom, I thought—had moved every piece of furniture and knickknack.

Memories and flashbacks followed me through the house like a string of magnetic ducks trailing a child from room to room. I placed dots on random items. As I passed Dave's room, I wondered if his stack of porn magazines was still on the top shelf of his closet. My body tingled. Damn, the pull was still there.

I quickly moved to my office-bedroom. Holding my breath, I walked in and stared at a room stripped of my presence. The box of children's books in a corner was the only thing left of me. I handed the box to Vicki and closed the door on that part of my life.

The master bedroom looked the same. Opening my dresser's top drawer, I reached to the back. I didn't find the baby bottle or pacifier that had started this whole nightmare. The last of my secrets had been uncovered. I didn't care or remember what was in the other drawers or closet. I only knew I wanted to get out of this room that held so much pain.

Penny appeared in the hallway just as I was about to leave—tail wagging, eyes bright.

"Penny!" I cried. "Where's my girl been?"

Sitting on the floor, I buried my tear-streaked face in her fur. "I'm so sorry I left you. I didn't mean to. I was supposed to be back home in three months."

Her fur felt like heaven. Her tongue on my face was like the kiss of angels. I cried for having left her and for where my life had taken me. She was warm, alive, and trusting. I wanted to stay wrapped in her essence forever, but I knew that wasn't possible. She wanted out of my arms, and I needed to get out of the home that was no longer mine.

I took one last look around before leaving for good. Then I headed back to the foyer. Once there, my eyes drifted up to the top of the stairs where Penny stood watching me. Slowly, I climbed a few steps and kissed her on the nose. "I love you, Mommy's girl, and always will."

I don't remember my return trip to the unit because I chose to accept a purple Xanax from Vicki, but when I exited the car, I recalled the sadness in Dave's eyes. It was the last time I'd see him until divorce court.

# Chapter 23

## *Murder?*

"Good morning, cutie," Dr. Bobbi said as she hugged me and pointed to her cheeks for a kiss. "Are you ready to build?"

I nodded and picked up Baby, and off to the sand room we went.

"Whatcha going to build today?"

I shrugged because I was just playing. I built these trays based on my "hypnosis" sessions, previous trays, dining room gossip, and pure imagination.

Braun never participated in my sand tray sessions, and neither did my nurses—only Dr. Bobbi. No one heard or objected to her leading questions.

My usual objects went into the sand first: a cross placed upside down, a few shiny red glass stones, and a green plastic coffin.

"Good," she said. "I see you're building a cult scene today. What's next?"

The black-winged plastic action figures were next. I put them in a circle and then decided to see what Bobbi would say if I stacked them on top of one another as if they were having sex. I felt my body respond. Shit, I guess that compulsion's not cured, I thought.

"Interesting," she said. "Go on. What's next?"

It's hard to say exactly when I gave in to what Dr. Braun and Dr. Bobbi were suggesting. It felt like one day I was just playing in the sand for fun, and the next, I was exhausted from fighting a battle I couldn't win. Growing up, I'd never heard the word *cult*. To me, it carried no fear or sense of danger. All I knew at that point was they were sure I had participated in one. I felt I had to play their game their way, or my life would get a lot worse than it already was.

If they wanted to see cult scenes, I'd provide them. It was a win-win situation: I got the approval I needed, and the doctors gained their fame.

Yet, while I built, my mind raced. What might a cult ceremony look like? What would someone hear or feel? I was told during hypnosis sessions that the cult did horrific things like blood sacrifices. So that's what I portrayed as I anticipated the attention and praise I would receive.

The idea that babies would be next sparked my imagination. Sex meant babies, and my mind reasoned that those babies would grow up and join cult ceremonies. They would be brainwashed— just like I was being brainwashed every second I was held captive in this unit.

There were many tiny plastic babies on the shelf to choose from. I randomly picked up a few and set them next to the black action figures.

"Ah," Dr. Bobbi said casually, her eyes wide. "Did you conceive a baby from that ceremony?"

Huh? Where did that come from? I thought.

"No. I've told you before I've never been pregnant."

"No? Well, let's see what your fingers have to say. Give me your hand, please."

I liked finger signals. Dr. Bobbi would hold and stroke my hand. But I also hated them because my "yes" finger kept moving more often than my "no" finger. Even when I said no or something wasn't true, my "yes" finger would contradict me and respond with a yes.

A few years after my discharge, a therapist and office manager at Bobbi's private practice told me she knew Bobbi didn't use finger signals correctly.

"Finger signals require more observation skills than Bobbi had," she said. "They are always paired with hypnosis and questions that can only be answered with yes or no. Bobbi broke that rule by asking you leading questions."

"I knew by the look on her face and the tone of her voice how I should respond," I'd replied. "A yes always felt like a required answer."

"I have no doubt you felt that way," she said, "but a trained therapist can tell when a client is faking their signals by observing unconscious movements like twitches or head nods. From what I gathered, you were easily swayed and eager to please, so more than likely, Bobbi programmed your fingers to always say yes. And for that, I remain appalled."

As my hand joined Dr. Bobbi's open palm, a cold shiver ran through my body.

"Did you or someone inside you ever conceive a baby during a cult ceremony?"

Suddenly, I felt like I was on shaky ground. I was sure I could make my no finger rise. But it didn't. Before I could figure out what was going on, she asked, "Can you show me what happened next?"

My stomach cramped. It was hard to breathe. "No, I'm making this all up."

"I think you do know," she said, taking her hand away. "It's right here in the sand."

I couldn't think straight. My guts twisted tighter. By now I knew when I couldn't wiggle out of doing what was asked.

I was alone since I had stopped asking for God's help. I took a deep breath, set a long table in the sand, placed candles on each end, and carefully balanced a silver bread-knife replica on the edge of the table.

"Is that a sacrificial altar?"

"No!" I hesitated, then blurted, "No, the cult members are going to have a sort of communion after their...ah...ceremony?" It didn't make sense, but it was the only explanation my panicky mind could come up with.

She grabbed my hand and repeated the question. "Is that a sacrificial altar?"

"No, it's not," I said again as my "yes" finger responded.

She didn't ask, What is it then? She knew she had me, and that's all that mattered.

Dr. Bobbi sighed—a deeper sound with an edge that made my blood run cold. "What did you have to do?"

"Nothing."

"I know this is hard. Show me. Show me now. What did you have to do!"

"No, I can't." Still, I felt compelled to please, so like the programmed robot I was, I picked up a baby and a few shiny red glass stones and placed them on the damning plastic table. Then I froze.

"Excellent, you're doing so well. Now tell me, did you have to sacrifice that baby?"

"No! No! Noooooooo!" I cried, pulling away from Dr. Bobbi and hiding my hands behind my back.

"We've discussed your pregnancy before, Linda, and I know you've denied it, but now it's time to tell me if you ever had to sacrifice your babies. Remember, you will never get well if you keep denying everything."

She'd upped the ante. Braun had threatened to send me to Elgin Mental Health Center the last time I refused to take my meds. Elgin was run by the state and known as a dreadful, overcrowded asylum. Only the worst cases were admitted, and you were damn lucky to return to society with all your marbles— if you were fortunate enough to leave at all.

Would Dr. Bobbi threaten the same thing? I no longer knew who I was. Fear wrapped me like a caterpillar's cocoon. My very essence was being forced into the messy goop stage. The question remained: would I emerge believing I was a victim of satanic ritual abuse, or would I come out as a victim of *their* insane abuse? I had no idea.

My babies? How did we get here? Anger bubbled up through my morning cocktail of meds. I wanted to scream, What part of no don't you understand?

"None of this is true. I take back everything," I stammered, shaking my head violently. "I'm just putting dollhouse toys in a sand tray. I'd have known if I were pregnant! Dammit, I would remember."

"No, you wouldn't. I'm sorry—we can discuss this later. You've had a lot to take in today."

This was more than I had ever imagined. The stakes had risen and spiraled out of control. Yet in a sad way, I finally felt special. It seemed like my entire life I'd craved recognition. I wanted something extraordinary to point to when someone called me dumb or stupid. I'd never achieved that before, but now I had. I was on a special unit with special doctors, and I was made to believe I was one of the most abused cases they'd ever seen. But that turned out to be false too. Everyone who interacted with Braun and Sachs was led to believe they alone were their worst case.

I was being accused of murder. Dr. Bobbi didn't call it that, but I could no longer correctly process what was being asked of me. It felt like murder. Sacrifice? Murder? Weren't they the same? This was serious. If they could convince the authorities I'd killed babies, couldn't I go to prison?

With tears streaming down my face, my fear and anger intensified. My body felt like a blacktop road radiating heat waves on a scorching summer day. Every second in this hospital was worsening, and I was dangerously close to knocking the entire sand tray off its stand. I wanted to see it shatter into thousands of pieces on the floor, but I knew that wouldn't solve anything and might get me sent to QR 1. So, with my hands clenched tightly, I said through gritted teeth, "If I had lots of pregnancies and killed babies, then I need proof. I want a pelvic exam."

"Oh, you do, do you?" Dr. Bobbi's eyebrows shot up.

"Yes. An exam will show I've never been pregnant."

The sand room fell into a deadly silence as we both stared at each other. Enough was enough. I didn't trust Braun for a second and was sure that if I pushed him too far, he'd turn me over to the police in an instant.

It took a few minutes, but I finally heard, "I'll talk to Buddy. I'll have Kate bring you a Xanax while you put the toys back on the shelf. Now, give me a hug, and I'll stop by later."

I foolishly expected to be examined in a private office. But once again, I was wrong. Instead, some skinny doctor with a long white lab coat came into my room with Dr. Bobbi.

"Let's see what we have here," she said.

It felt so incongruous. With legs spread wide, I wondered what this doctor would think if she knew that under my crisp white bedspread lay Becky's bright alphabet sheets.

The actual exam was a blur, but the results were not. "Yes," the doctor said to Dr. Bobbi, who was watching from the far end of the room. "I've seen many cases of cervical trauma from pregnancies and forced abortions. Hers is no different."

"Sorry, dearie," she said to me. "But the good thing now is you're safe."

Dearie? Safe? From what—or whom? Was I safe from going to jail? Where the hell did they find this doctor, and how much was she paid to say what was necessary to keep this pregnancy insanity going?

I knew then I would never be able to trust anyone again, and I was furious. I had denied being part of a cult whenever I dared to defy my doctors. But as it turned out, that wasn't true. Right here, right now, I was in a cult—one I had no idea how to escape from.

"You look ready to explode," Dr. Bobbi said. "Would you like to go to the padded quiet room to let off some steam?"

I'd never been in QR 2, but letting off steam sounded necessary. "I never had a baby. That doctor lied."

"Let's go," Dr. Bobbi said.

QR 2 was a padded room no larger than a walk-in closet. A well-worn tan beanbag chair and a pillow sat in the corner. The dim lighting made me feel as if I were removed from the world. There was just me, Dr. Bobbi, and an overwhelming amount of anger.

She shut the door, handed me the soft white pillow, then dropped her large body into the beanbag chair and said, "Go for it. Let it out."

My initial attempts were weak. I was afraid of losing control and never coming back to reality. Still, my fiery anger was stronger than my fear, and as I hammered the pillow on the floor and hit the padded walls, I gained momentum.

"Not true, not true," escalated into screams interspersed with, "I've never had any babies. None. Do you fucking hear me? None, none, none! None of this goddamned stuff is true. That fake doctor lied, lied, lied!"

Repeatedly, I beat the padded walls, swore, and sobbed for everything that had gone wrong and for everything I couldn't say that still imprisoned me. I was so close to losing touch with reality.

I wept for not being believed, for not being able to say goodbye to my father, for a mother I hated and who scared me, for the loss of Penny, for not feeling real love for another person, for the sex stuff that made no sense, for wanting to die so badly I could taste the brimstone of hell, for lying my ass off, and for being in this hellhole being told I'd had babies and sacrificed them.

I started to run out of breath and slid to the ground. But I wasn't done.

I pulled myself up and repeatedly beat the pillow on the floor until I was so exhausted I couldn't move. I had no voice left. I had no strength left. I had no life left as I once again collapsed into a sobbing mess, lying in horrendous pain on the dirty floor of the padded room.

Dr. Bobbi let me lie there for a while, then pulled me onto her lap and ran her fingers through my hair. "You did a good job getting your feelings out," she said while rocking me. "This is tough stuff you're facing right now. But I don't think you can take much more, so I'll talk to Buddy about giving you some relief."

It took both Vicki and Dr. Bobbi to get me back to my room and into pajamas. Dr. Bobbi tucked me into bed with Baby while Vicki waited for the promised relief to arrive.

It came as a pill that only Braun could administer. "Dr. Bobbi and I believe you need a time-out, so I'm giving you chloral hydrate. It's a harmless sedative that dentists sometimes use for dental procedures. It will help relieve your anxiety and, hopefully, allow you to have a deep sleep."

The drug didn't do what Braun said it would. Instead of making me sleepy and less anxious, I got tipsy. I couldn't walk a straight line to the bathroom, giggled at the nurses' hellos, and entertained myself by making Baby do somersaults down my sheets. Once again, I spent the night near the nursing station—this time higher than a kite.

The next day, back in my room, my anger returned with new drive. I opened every book I had brought from home and tore out the page with the bookplate that read *This book belongs to Linda Cooper.* I then tore those pages into tiny pieces and tossed them into my trash can, stepping on them like grapes as if I were making fine wine.

If I couldn't physically kill myself, I would do it symbolically. When I was sure everything associated with Linda's name was gone, I made my final act of defiance. I ripped off my hospital bracelet, placed it on top of the trampled pieces, and carried the can to the nursing station. Setting it on the desk, I quietly said to the wide-eyed nurse, "Please tell everyone that from now on, I will only answer to the name Lyn. Linda is officially dead."

# Chapter 24

## *Guessing Games*

I was issued a new hospital bracelet, and the staff did call me Lyn, but as I suspected, it didn't make any difference in my daily life. Becky and I continued to operate as a seamless team.

As Becky, I played with preschool puzzles, colored, and sang nursery rhymes. She kept the horror and incredible pain and confusion of hospital life at a distance.

During the morning, the adult me created elaborate scenes in the sand tray. Dr. Bobbi stopped watching my building process. Instead, she took Polaroids after I finished. She made the photos sound necessary, and I felt important. Some she gave to me, others she kept. I now assume they were added to my chart to prove to my insurance company that I was a danger to myself and others. I never knew what to do with mine. I didn't need more reminders of what I hadn't done.

I wasn't one to socialize and tended to keep to myself. Nevertheless, I was good at assessing which new patient would need extra attention or who had an ax to grind.

Karen arrived in my third year, and I sensed she would be a handful. Her thin arms stuck out of a misaligned, button-down, long-sleeved shirt. Her uneven, flame-red hair looked like she had cut it herself with blunt scissors. Her dark eyes constantly darted everywhere, which indicated to me she could bolt at any moment.

I was right. She escaped once, then again. The third time she slipped through the locked doors as a visitor arrived, it was her last. Her transfer to a higher-security ward was immediate.

The next day, Kate brought me a list of about fifteen names.

"Dr. Braun would like you to circle the names on this list that look familiar to you."

Shit—Braun is on another fact-finding mission, I thought. He'd ask various patients the same questions to see how many gave him matching answers. "Circle which cult holiday is correct," or "what does this cult symbol mean?" I circled and filled in the blanks on many of Braun's lists. It was like playing a multiple-choice game. These questions also gave me an idea of what details Dr. Bobbi would try to pull out of me during therapy sessions.

Braun's twisted interpretation of the meaning of flowers was the hardest on us as patients. I'd just come back from lunch and was writing in my journal about my brick-hard toasted-cheese sandwich with soggy fries when Braun burst into my room. He stepped so close I could see his nose hairs.

"Is it true that if a cult member receives red roses and white baby's breath from a family member, it means a bloody suicide, as opposed to pink roses and baby's breath, which means a hanging?"

My eyes widened and my fingers stiffened like they did when I was scared out of my mind. I hated these interrogations that made no logical sense. What the hell was he talking about? These weren't Victorian times when flowers conveyed secret messages. His question hung in the air as I tried to find a way to squirm out of answering. But I knew there was no way out, so I told him he was right.

The smirk on his face was enormous as he asked the next million-dollar question. "Does the receiver need to kill herself upon receiving the bouquet?"

I wasn't surprised. So many of Dr. Bobbi and Braun's

accusations and cult beliefs revolved around death. "Sure," I said, slowly blowing out my held breath. "That's true too."

"Bingo," he said, looking like he'd just won the grand prize on Jeopardy.

Within days, all flowers sent to patients were returned. Flowers of any kind, along with greeting cards and letters, were banned because, according to Braun, secret code words and messages were being relayed to the recipients.

I quickly scanned the names that Kate brought to me. I knew no one on this new game sheet, but I circled six random names and handed it back.

I thought I was done. But I was wrong. With the usual scowl on his face, Braun practically flew into my room.

"Don't you ever tell me you've never been in a cult. You've just confirmed you know the names of some of the biggest suspected cult leaders in Chicago."

My heart raced, making my head feel like furniture was being shuffled around. "But I just guessed at the names," I said, grabbing Baby. "You know, like multiple choice. I don't know any of those people."

"You can't deny this, Lyn. Before Karen left the unit, she confirmed the same names that Jerry Smith, a Chicago cop, had given me. He's convinced there are satanic cults in Chicago. Also, Karen mentioned she's seen you at ceremonies."

Braun looked so damn pleased with himself, like he finally had the proof he needed to justify keeping me in his unit as long as possible. I hugged Baby as waves of fear crashed through me. Braun held my fate in his hands. He was an arrogant bastard. Now it was clear he not only had a warped mind but also had power and the ears of the Chicago Police Department. I'd felt his anger when I was lucid enough to deny him the information he wanted, and I'd seen him dress down a nurse outside a patient's room. I could be toast if he decided to turn me over to the police for questioning about illegal cult activities. I clung to the hope that Dr. Bobbi wouldn't let that happen, yet I could feel my mind spiraling with thousands of "what ifs."

Despite—or maybe because of—the shock, there was a frightening stillness inside as I pictured slitting Braun's throat. I kept building scenes of bloody sacrifices in the sand. It would be so easy. But would it? Jesus, I silently screamed, how in God's holy name could you allow the head of this unit to lead a mentally disturbed woman into believing she is part of a cult, had babies, participated in perverse sexual acts, and now, dear Mother of God, feel like she could really be capable of murder?

"Who's here?" Braun asked. "Did you hear what I said?"

"Yes, I heard," I said. "But it's not true."

Staring at me, he said, "I think your switching is getting out of control. I'll be increasing your Inderal and adding a med."

"But I don't want any more meds, and besides, there's no one else inside me." Braun's lips pursed like they always did when I denied being multiple, so I knew I was pushing it, but I didn't care.

"Damn it. Don't I have a choice?"

"Yes—your choice is either you take your meds or get taken to QR."

"What kind of choice is that?" I asked as my voice rose and my fingers stiffened again. "Either way, I have to take meds I don't want."

"It's the only choice you have. Think about it and have a good day."

As his flying coattails left my room, I gave him the finger multiple times, then made a vow. I would spit out the next foreign med that appeared in my little white cup, even if it did mean being put in restraints while in QR 1. I'd been there before and survived. I could do it again.

# Chapter 25

## *Abreactions*

A breaction therapy was first used in the early 20th century to help traumatized soldiers. The theory was that if soldiers could re-experience their memories, they would be able to talk about them. Despite early promise, psychoanalysts found that dredging up feelings without a clear understanding of what was happening inside a person's mind didn't work. Drs. Braun and Bobbi either ignored this research or decided it was acceptable to keep using the outdated method.

All of us "cult multiples" were supposedly suffering from traumatic, dissociated memories. According to Braun, these memories were hidden in our unconscious by alters who were afraid to reveal their experiences. After information was extracted from us through hypnotism, sand trays, or artwork, the next step was abreaction therapy. We were told that abreactions were the only way we could heal.

These sessions were supposed to "normalize" what we did and allow us to talk about our crimes without dissociating or wanting to kill ourselves. Then our alternate personalities would integrate back into the host personality and eventually disappear because they would no longer be needed. We would be on the road to recovery—becoming whole.

Patients were in an impossible spot. Therapists who met Braun at conferences were anxious to have their clients admitted to his specialized unit, so there was a waiting list. Braun's evaluation was the end of the line for most of us desperate souls seeking answers. We were willing to believe the unbelievable because we thought we were being evaluated and treated by the very best.

It wasn't until the very end that I realized I was being held captive in this cult-like facility because of my insurance. My benefits were extensive, with no limits on hospital stays.

These therapists who attended Braun's conferences saw the doctors at Rush as gods worth waiting for. Drs. Braun and Bobbi had years of "knowledge" and experience—but were they worth the wait? No. Their unit was built around a fabricated phenomenon that spun out of control, leading to confusion and heartbreak. Families were broken apart, and in some cases, their unethical therapy resulted in suicide.

What happened during treatment was shocking and immoral. Everyone received the same diagnosis, and as I watched this happen over and over, I wondered if they all believed what they were told. Did we all think we could commit such terrible acts? Or were we too scared to speak up, thinking, who am I to question the best doctors in the world? We even had a group from the Netherlands visit our unit, and we acted like good little patients. Becky read them a story in her sweet little voice while the visitors smiled and looked impressed. Our doctors were supposedly on the cutting edge and, in the world's eyes, could do no wrong.

I remember the morning Dr. Bobbi breezed into my room and plopped her purse behind my bed. I was entering my fourth year at Rush, and I now believe my insurance benefits had been calculated to the penny. Therapy was becoming less about what I "did" in the cult and more about how I was handling what I had supposedly done. The team wanted more of me and less of my child persona, Becky.

I had Dr. Bobbi's coffee ready. I loved the thought that I was doing something to please her. The coffee also ensured she would see me the moment she arrived on the unit. After her first sip and hug, she said, "You won't be building today. Your team has decided it's time for you to own what you have been putting in the sand these past years. You'll never be able to function in society if this 'it's not true' business doesn't stop."

"But it's not true," I started to say, which made Dr. Bobbi sigh and put on her caring face.

"You are strong enough now to act out what you had to do, Lyn. This is called abreaction therapy, and it's the next step to your owning what you had to do."

My heart sank. I didn't know exactly how these sessions worked, but every patient knew when they took place. The screams that bled through the closed door were unavoidable. Some of us prayed for whoever was on the hot seat. Some stayed in their rooms with pillows over their heads. Others turned up the TV in the common room, knowing the screams would stop eventually. I usually held Baby tightly and sang as loudly as I could.

Now it was my turn. Dr. Bobbi and I agreed I would act out sacrificing an animal because that was supposed to be less painful than the other things I had allegedly been forced to do.

"Let's start in the beanbag chairs," she said as she closed the door to the padded room. "Do you have the alters gathered that participated in sacrificing animals?"

"I guess," I said, wringing my hands.

"Good. We'll start with hypnosis. Now, everybody listen."

When she reached ten and I confirmed that "everyone" was present, Bobbi continued, "What you all had to do was terrible—something no one should ever have to go through. I want you to get out of your beanbag chair and have someone show me what you had to do. When this is over, you can integrate those alters into your body, knowing you will never have to do that again."

My heart raced. Please, God, I don't want to do this. Can't you just take me now? Please.

The small room felt claustrophobic. My hands and rigid

fingers twisted in the air. I could hear my heart beating wildly in my ears.

"How can I act out something I never did?" I whispered.

"Stop it, Lyn. Step aside and let the alters responsible come forward."

"I can't. I don't know how to hold a sacrificial knife."

"No, you don't, Lyn. But someone inside does. Tell me—was it night or day when you sacrificed animals?"

My mind scrambled for a plausible scenario. Who would conduct a sacrificial ceremony in broad daylight? It had to be night—right? I hoped I guessed correctly. "Night?"

"Good. Do you hear a cat meow?"

I held my breath. I now had a gut-wrenching sense of why screams came from this room where all that was supposedly unspeakable was revealed.

This, for me, was the scariest and most upsetting part. I made up scenes five days a week, but I didn't have to show how I did it. Was I supposed to slit the cat's throat or stab it in the heart? Was there a specific procedure? Were there chants? How were we dressed—or were we naked?

I must get this right, I thought, slipping into an old, familiar childhood fear of displeasing my mom. When I made my bed in the morning, Mom would often remake it. "You didn't do it right," she'd say with an angry face. Mom was left-handed. When it was my turn to set the table, her knife had to be on the left. If I forgot and put it on the right, it could set her off. I never knew when she'd go bonkers. Spit would gather in the corners of her mouth as she called me "dumb" and "stupid," followed by, "Why can't you ever do anything right?" Her spontaneous rages frightened me to the core, which only caused me to make more mistakes.

I felt the same deep fear as I stalled for time. What if, after all these years, Bobbi realized I knew nothing about how cults operate? She had sessions with patients every day. In my mind, she understood how cults worked. If I did things wrong, would she get angry and threaten to send me away like my mother had? I was too old for an orphanage, but there were other places I could be sent. I was terrified of acting this out the "wrong" way.

"Go on, Lyn—show me what you had to do."

My mind madly searched for what to do next. I pretended to pick up a tiny kitten. I mimed petting it.

"I can't do this. I can't."

"Yes, you can. If you don't, you will die," Bobbi said in her harsh *I mean it* voice.

My hands trembled as I mimed placing an imaginary kitten on a pretend cult altar. I lit a candle, and as the imaginary flame flickered, I felt the inside of my head shift with it.

I was no longer in QR.

The candlelight flickered brightly in a dark room. I felt naked. Afraid to glance down to see if it was true, I stared straight ahead.

"Go on—what happened next?"

Slowly, I mimed picking up a knife and made stabbing and chopping motions. Everything felt surreal. An acrid smell filled my nostrils and I wanted to puke. I knew I had never done these awful things, but in that moment I could see, feel, and almost taste what I was being accused of doing. The more I acted it out, the more real it felt.

The imaginary blood was hot and sticky. I felt hands caress my blood-spattered body, and I could see the tiny warm kitten now as a cold, bloody lump of red fur. Bile rose. Tears fell. I had reached the fires of hell.

"What did you want to do to those leaders, Lyn? What do you want to tell those people who made you do these things?"

My stomach churned. I didn't move—couldn't move. Dr. Bobbi's voice seemed distant. Why was she asking questions that had no answers? As the scene slowly faded, I stood frozen, dissociated, with the words she wanted stuck deep inside.

"Come back, Lyn," she kept saying. "The reenactment is over. Come back. You don't ever have to do this again."

I didn't believe her.

I heard the screams in my head before they escaped my frozen body. They felt primal. I was driven by instinct. What I had endured was barbaric in every way. I knew I had to answer her questions—one way or another, this team always got what they wanted.

Words poured out in both a child's and an adult's voice. "Me's wants to frow up. Me's needs my cwothes back on. Everything smells like poop. I want this sticky blood off, off, off. I want this kitten to be alive again. I want to kill my mommy for bringing me here and all the leaders for making me do these things. And God, please, I want to die now—because none of this is true."

Today, I would compare this to watching an animal sacrifice through a virtual-reality headset. I believe the panic I felt while acting out this ritual caused a hallucination. Day after day, I had put blood and horror into my trays. I didn't read novels. I had limited access to the outside world. I didn't watch TV or read newspapers. Xanax was like candy. The Halcion that caused dark, swirling dreams didn't wear off until noon. The Inderal was reaching dangerous levels.

Seeing visions of what wasn't there was bound to happen. But the "reality" of what I saw made me fear Drs. Braun and Bobbi had finally broken me and I was losing my grip on knowing I was innocent.

Once the abreaction was over, Dr. Bobbi brought me back into her lap. I couldn't be calmed. The integration process she wanted to guide me through wasn't possible. I was too far gone. That would have to wait until the next day.

My screams had been heard. The halls were empty when I was taken back to my room. Two white Xanax and a Halcion waited for me. Suicide precautions were in place: my bed rails were raised, and I was tucked in with Baby. Dr. Bobbi and Vicki took turns staying with me until I passed out from exhaustion and too many meds.

These sessions happened several times a month. They never became easier. Bobbi did get "smarter" and placed a peach Xanax under my tongue before sessions began. It dulled some of the intensity, but the work remained psychologically brutal.

The worst session was acting out the delivery of my imaginary babies. Bobbi decided these nightmares should take place on the bed in my room. Never having experienced labor—and not knowing how anyone could survive something so devastating—I was frozen with fear even before we began. She had stopped using hypnosis for these sessions, but she did ask if I had all my alters ready. I confirmed they were present and we could proceed.

I lay on my back. The white bedspread felt too clean and bright for delivering and sacrificing a baby. I heard, "Open your legs and spread them apart." Questions started. Dr. Bobbi stood over me. She touched me between my legs. I closed my eyes. Maybe if I didn't look at her, she'd stop. More questions. I felt her hand and arm rubbing across the crotch of my brown slacks. More made-up details of how the babies were delivered and taken from me came into my head. I moaned. I screamed. Her hands rubbed and pressed hard on my vagina. I squirmed. I felt a familiar tingle and wanted to have an orgasm. We fell into a rhythm. She moved with me. Nothing resembled any delivery I had ever seen on TV. Would this ever end? Moments before my desire became a reality, she stopped. The abreaction was "complete."

What's complete? Had I just imagined that my "doctor"—my mommy—had been sexually inappropriate with me? What happened felt wrong. But who was I going to tell?

Dr. Bobbi treated me as she always did after an abreaction. I was given another Xanax and congratulated for a job well done, which made me wonder who the liar really was. I'd told a whopper. My description of how babies were born, taken, and sacrificed didn't make sense—not even to me. Anyone with a questioning mind would have seen holes bigger than Mexico's Copper Canyon.

But was Bobbi lying too? Today, I think both of us were caught up in our own lies for our own reasons. Coming clean came with too many consequences. Bobbi and I were entangled in a web so deep and complicated, nothing could have broken us apart.

I made a journal entry before the second Xanax kicked in and dulled the reality of what had happened in the name of therapy. Every experience seemed watered down. The drugs and how they were administered always robbed me of the ability to process and understand the enormously unethical tactics they were using.

But I wanted to record this experience. I wrote everything down—where I was, what I remember saying, where I felt her hands. I longed for an orgasm but didn't get one. I kept writing until my eyes wouldn't stay open anymore, and my only choice was to lie down on the same bed that, a short time ago, had been stained with blood and baby parts. That didn't feel right either, so I let the Xanax carry me to a place of nothingness, hoping I'd never come back.

The next morning, as usual, Dr. Bobbi picked up my journal and started to read. "You will rip this up immediately," she said. "I did not touch you." I now believe she knew what she had done was wrong and didn't want to risk anyone else finding out. Her denial was too quick, too firm, too final. I did what I was told. Then I stared at the ragged pieces scattered on the floor. They resembled how I felt—destroyed and torn apart. How I wished I could wipe out my entire memory bank of hospital experiences by simply ripping up every notebook I had ever written in.

After this, I sat quietly and pretended to have integrations. These were peaceful sessions, almost like meditation. It was easy to say I accepted what this or that alter had to do because, in my mind, I held the truth: they had never been there in the first place. For once, I didn't have to lie when I said, "Yes, they are gone."

Dr. Bobbi always said she was proud of me and promised that if I kept working hard, I had a small chance of being released back into society. It was a tentative promise, but one I clung to with every ounce of sanity I had left.

# Chapter 26

## *Name Change*

A few days before my last birthday at Rush, Braun arrived in my room. I'd soon be 43, but I still felt like plain old four. I wasn't in the mood for the "Happy Birthday–Merry Christmas" greetings I'd be getting, but I still managed to dress both Baby and me in red and green.

"I have some news I think you'll like," he said. "We've heard from your husband. Your divorce is scheduled for April. We're permitting you to meet with a lawyer to review your terms."

It took a few seconds to sink in. I barely remembered I was still legally married. Penny sometimes entered my mind, but she never stayed long.

"Divorced, like no longer married?"

"Yes. That's what you wanted, isn't it?"

"I don't have a lawyer."

"Your husband has seen that you do."

I was surprised, yet leery. Was this just a tease?

"But," said Braun.

I knew it. "What's the "but?"

"The *but* is, I strongly think you need to consider changing your full name at the time of divorce. It won't cost you anything if you do it then."

"Why would I want to do that?"

"I thought about having you enrolled in the witness protection program, but after Dr. Bobbi and I talked, we decided a name change would be better."

"I still don't understand."

"You must be extremely careful when you're released, because it's my guess the cult will come looking for you. Members will try to lure you back. It's happened to others."

Here it was again. I hadn't belonged to a cult when my dad died. I didn't belong to one now, so how could a cult find me and take me back? This defied belief. Why would they want me? As far as I knew, no one had ever called or tried to send flowers to hush me up. Was all this talk Braun's paranoia? Bobbi had told me Braun was sure he was being followed.

"Exposing cults is dangerous business," he said. "Vicki will fill you in. Have a good day."

My face lit up brighter than the fake Christmas tree on the top shelf at the nurses' station. Divorce and the possibility of getting back to having a life of my own? Wow—Happy Birthday and Merry Christmas to me!

The thought of changing my name was intriguing. All I heard when someone called me "Linda" was the "duh," as in "duh, you're so dumb."

I am eight, maybe nine, sitting at our scratched dining room table. My father is across from me, pulling money from his pockets. Coins rattle across the shiny surface. His face is angry. My homework is to solve five math story problems. They all involve how much money or how many marbles kids have at the end of the story. These problems always confuse me and make me anxious.

I've asked Mom for help, but she said, "Ask your father. He's good with money." I ask. And even with the coins stacked in front of me, I still get the answer wrong. His voice is loud and harsh. "How can you be so dumb?" I freeze and remain silent.

That day, with that one word—"dumb," spoken so forcefully

—my father affirmed what I already suspected. I was dumb when I couldn't pass tests. I was dumb when I couldn't make friends. I was dumb when I didn't know how to live in my own skin or meet expectations. "Dumb" defined me as a less-than child who would never amount to anything. And the sad part was that I believed him.

I took Braun's convoluted thinking to heart. I would change my name to something that wouldn't remind me I was dumb every time I heard or wrote it. It took a few days, but just as I'd had the memory of my dad, I remembered attending a baby shower. The woman was having a girl and naming her *Jamie*. As I wrote various names in my journal, *Jamie* kept floating to the top. I liked the sound of *me* in *Jamie*. It didn't sound like *duh*, and it satisfied my desperate desire to belong to myself. Jamie it was.

I also felt strongly about using *Lyn* as my middle name—it would keep some connection to my birth name. Choosing a last name was hardest. Nothing sounded right until I remembered a psychic reading. "To step into who you are," the psychic had said, "your name should be Dulce Marie Weaver." I didn't like *Dulce* or *Marie*, but I loved *Weaver*. Weaver was a job description. Yes— when the time came, I would become Jamie Lyn Weaver, weaving together my new life. Lovely.

The following month, I met my appointed lawyer. Vicki asked if I wanted her to be present. Holding onto details was difficult for me, so I agreed. A second set of ears would help.

When the day came, the adult me was present. My hair was combed and curled. A clean sweater and too-big jeans hung around my waist. Other than being surprised at how thin I'd become, I appeared normal. Inside, though, my stomach was tying itself in knots.

"When you have signed and agreed to the terms, this will go back to Dave's lawyer," the attorney said. "The divorce grounds indicate the respondent (you) has been guilty of extreme and repeated mental cruelty toward the petitioner (Dave)."

Expected, though still stinging. I felt lower than a speck of dust. I wished someone would blow me into nothingness. After everything was explained, I was consumed with guilt. I'd be receiving money from our joint savings account and 70 percent of the proceeds from the sale of our home. In addition, Dave would pay alimony for thirty-six months after I was discharged.

Never in my wildest dreams did I think I'd be so well provided for. Dave and I had never talked about what the divorce would entail. I thought all I'd have were my green dotted items. Glancing at Vicki for approval, I asked, "Can I change my entire name at the time of divorce?"

"I'll have the papers drawn up."

Later, when Vicki came to check on me, I told her I was blown away by what I'd be receiving.

"I did caution Dave that your chances of functioning on your own were slim to none," she said. "He's a good guy, and I believe he still cares for you."

That hurt too.

More hope arrived with this second mention of a release. It came with the same caution I'd hear repeatedly: "Make sure no one is following you." When I promised I would, I was deemed ready to go outside without a nurse.

I started with short trips to Kmart with patients who needed personal items or an outing to grab a cigarette. An aide drove us in a small van. We had one hour and were warned that if we got into trouble or didn't return on time, we'd lose all privileges. At first, I caught the aide following me. When she saw I was aware of my surroundings and could be trusted not to bolt, she left me alone to wander.

Mostly, those outings felt like torture. Too many people. Too much visual stimulation. I just wanted to grab what I needed and get the hell out. But I had to wait until the hour was up.

Eventually, Becky and I found our way to the toy department.

Standing in front of the vast selection of games and glittery art supplies, I became aware for the first time that I had no control over the alter my mind had created to preserve my sanity. Becky and I talked out loud constantly on the unit—like a ventriloquist chatting with his puppet. Becky told me what she was thinking or wanted in her voice, and I answered back in mine. I assumed she'd go away once I left the hospital. But she didn't. She was now intrinsically intertwined with my psyche.

Becky had a quirky way of sticking out the tip of her tongue as she spoke in her own vocabulary. She walked with her hands and fingers in motion, and developed her own likes and dislikes. She held my sense of wonder and joy. Her purpose, it seemed, was to step in whenever anything became too overwhelming. Like Kmart.

While there, I felt like I was in a foreign country where everyone spoke a language I didn't understand. Within minutes of arriving, Becky was front and center saying, "Me needs new trayons and tollering boot."

"No, you don't. Dr. Bobbi gave you a new box of crayons last month, and you already have three coloring books."

"Pease?"

"Nope, kiddo. Can you go back inside, please?" I said, watching a mom steer her child away from me.

"Nooooo, yous needs me."

I hope that lady doesn't report me to the manager for being a nut case.

Is this what being free is going to be like? Because if it is, life is going to be far from normal.

# Chapter 27

## *Freedom?*

I t was bitterly cold the day Vicki and I arrived at the
courthouse for my divorce hearing. I was on suicide watch
again, and sucking on the Xanax Vicki had tucked under my
tongue. My raggedy jacket swished and my shoes squeaked on the
shiny floor as we entered a small courtroom. Even with Vicki
there, I felt alone. *This is it,* I thought—so simple, yet so complex.

Dave and his lawyer were already seated. Across the room he
looked like any other man in a suit and tie. But he wasn't any
man. He was someone I'd betrayed. Someone I couldn't love.
Someone I knew a lifetime ago.

The Xanax hit hard. I'd skipped breakfast, and Braun had
added a "happy pill" to my morning cocktail. The benches tilted
sideways, the room blurred, and what had felt unbearable a
minute earlier was now tolerable.

Rights were read. Our eyes met when I acknowledged the
divorce was uncontested, and again when Dave said he didn't
object to the terms. With a quick bang of the judge's gavel, on
April 4, 1989, a marriage that should never have happened was
legally over. I felt empty.

A month later, I officially became Jamie Lyn Weaver. It didn't
change anything. I was still a messed-up woman. Once the name

change was filed, things moved fast. Vicki introduced me to a friend who worked at a bank. She told him I was a satanic ritual abuse survivor, still very fragile, and "might not be able to transition back into society."

Oh yes I will, I thought. I didn't know how yet, but I'd do whatever it took to leave the loony bin where I'd been kept captive. Still, there were too many unknowns. We agreed I should set up a trust. Knowing I'd have alimony too eased my mind. If I was careful, I could build a new life.

By early June, Bobbi was vacationing in Alaska, and I was allowed outside alone. It was a big step. I had just returned to the unit when I heard, "Hey, cutie. I see you stayed safe while I was away. May I have my keychain back?"

I hugged her, kissed both cheeks, and pulled the heavy brass Tree of Life keychain from my sweater pocket.

Dr. Bobbi always gave me her keychain before trips. I had to promise to stay safe, not kill myself, and give it back to her in person.

"I have two presents for you," she said.

"Me too?" Becky asked.

"Yes, you too, Miss Becky," she said, ruffling my hair. "This one is for you."

Inside reindeer wrapping paper was a tiny Alaskan doll ornament made with fox and mink fur.

"Wow, fanks. Me woves her."

Dr. Bobbi beamed. "And you, Miss Jamie," she said, sitting beside me on the bed. "Your present is that it's time for you to leave the hospital."

"Leave—like now?"

"No, cutie. We don't have an exact date. Probably around when you came in—September."

"I'm well enough to be released?"

"You'll still need outpatient therapy, but your insurance policy is nearing its limit, and we want you to have some funds saved."

I had never asked how much these years had cost. Dave hadn't mentioned it and neither had anyone else.

"Um…how much do I—or did I—have?"

"Your policy has a million-dollar cap," she said without hesitation.

Stunned, I heard little after that. A million dollars, I kept thinking, and I'm reaching the limit. One million for a pack of lies and "memories" that turned my life upside down.

I'd watched women come and go and never wondered why I was allowed to stay so long. Dave worked for an insurance company. Our coverage was up to a million dollars each. I had assumed I was kept because I was more disturbed than the others. Not so. It was benefits, money, and their ambition. The diagnosis and the bill would follow me: higher premiums for years, because I might "relapse."

I was excited the end was near. But the thought of returning to society sent cold shivers down my spine. How was I supposed to tuck these years from hell back inside and function alone? It was drilled into me that I was a victim of a satanic cult and daily home abuse—and now I was supposed to be "better"?

No. Ninety-five percent of my day I was Becky. I still sometimes ate chicken and mashed potatoes with my fingers and ended up a mess. And Valerie—the sexual alter—was alive and active.

My compulsions were unpredictable. I could be reading to Becky one minute and the next, I'd be naked on my bed, writing porn with the door open and my fingers where they wanted to go. When I was caught or confessed, Braun called it "acting out cult programming." I'd stopped arguing. I promised to stop the exhibitionism, even though I knew I couldn't.

I no longer scanned the sky for exploding planes, but the compulsions were stronger. I had to count ceiling tiles to sixty-nine. If I miscounted, I started over. I looked for faces and animals in the particle board. I alphabetized my books by title. I dressed

Baby and myself in matching colors. It was painfully clear I would never get the diagnosis I'd gone in for.

The next three months flew. I built several more sand trays. The last one held hundreds of items. Dr. Bobbi said she wanted to videotape it and make a "training tape" on using sand trays for ritually abused patients—something to sell at conferences.

"You'll be helping others, Jamie. Your contribution will be invaluable."

If it was for training, I needed to say exactly what she wanted. And I did. I pointed to and explained sacrifices, hangings, blood baths, sexual orgies, and home abuse. At the end, in a tear-filled child's voice, I told my final lie: "The little girl who is me is standing on these coffins. Now she can finally look at and accept everything that happened to her."

Dr. Bobbi's smile was blinding as she hugged me. I had done what I was told, but I knew the tape was built on four years of lies. I wonder how many therapists bought it and then used it—never seeing the harm. Bobbi had no mental-health training. She was a gym teacher misusing sand tray therapy. I have a copy. It's one of the hardest things I've ever watched.

I asked to stop Halcion. The nightmares were worse, and I felt groggy past noon. Staff agreed. Everyone knew I was on dangerously high doses. I now believe they worried that if I requested those doses after discharge, someone might ask questions—something no one wanted.

My Inderal was tapered to a "reasonable" level. I later learned another Rush doctor not only approved but ignored Braun's requests for enormous amounts of medication. Today I wonder how much kickback money changed hands.

I quit Xanax cold turkey without telling anyone. I told myself I didn't need it, even though I craved the taste under my tongue and the way it dulled everything. Day one wasn't bad—furniture shifted in my head, which felt normal by then. I couldn't sleep. I blamed Halcion withdrawal. Day two brought anxiety. I paced the halls. By day three, with no sleep, my vision doubled and my skin crawled. I tried walking outside. It got worse. No depth perception. Clouds full of angry faces. Inside, I didn't feel real. Mickey-Mouse-like figures danced. Iridescent bugs marched across the ceiling. Withdrawal.

I desperately wanted a Xanax. For the first time, I truly pitied people addicted to hard drugs. Around day five, my skin settled and the images stopped moving. Sleep returned, and slowly I came back to life. When I could form sentences again, I asked a staffer to take me to the DMV to update my license. Dave had left my car in the hospital lot after the divorce.

Vicki had placed the keys in my top dresser drawer, next to my wedding ring and spending money. This locked drawer was used to store any personal items that could be stolen. When I was on serious suicide watches, I was forced to put my gold diamond-studded necklace in that drawer. Staff believed I could strangle myself with it.

Driving was a challenge. A two-hour refresher helped. Still, I startled at horns. At lights, I had to remember whether green meant stop or go. Becky chattered about everything she saw—distracting, but grounding.

Weekends I scanned the classifieds for apartments. I found a second-floor one-bedroom near the hospital that allowed pets. Vicki said my "also known as" papers were enough to sign a lease. I prayed the landlord wouldn't ask about the last four years. They didn't exist.

No one would tell me my release date, so I ferried books, clothes, and toys to the apartment a few hours each day. I had to return to the unit for meals and sleep "for insurance reasons."

Standing in my empty place, I was captivated by sunlight flooding the room. I opened and closed the windows just because I could. Outside, children played, a squirrel scrambled up a tree. Joy surged. No more "Mother, may I," I told the bare walls. I can use real silverware. A real knife. I cried at the beauty of it. Then terror returned in a flash. Could I live alone? Who would stop me if I wanted to harm myself? Who would hold me when I panicked over nothing? Would I keep exposing my body? A thousand questions, no answers.

I tired easily. Four years without exercise took a toll. I shopped in short bursts. First, I filled the fridge. Then the cabinets. Then furniture. When Becky sensed I'd had enough, she said, loud and clear, "Me needs to go home now pease."

Back at the unit, Vicki would ask if I'd been followed. "No," I'd say. She seemed relieved, then reminded me to stay vigilant. I could be abducted in an instant. The warnings never ended.

I still craved Xanax daily and sometimes asked for a few to savor under my tongue. But I wasn't eager to see bugs and cartoon figures again, so I resisted.

There was no celebration, which was fine. I hated parties. There was also no counseling on how to handle freedom. I'm not sure anyone believed I'd make it outside.

The day before discharge, I said goodbye to Kate, to Vicki, to the aides who kept me safe when I wanted to give up. I hadn't planned to cry, but I did. They had become family. I'd argued with some and defied others. Some had held my trembling body after sessions, others read me bedtime stories.

From the kitchen servers to the overnight aides, everyone wished me well and said they would miss Becky announcing it was a "dood morin."

Kate and Vicki gave me blue-and-white checked kitchen towels. Both said I could call the unit if I needed help. Vicki said she would see me in Braun's office for group therapy twice a month.

Braun warned me—again—to be careful who I talked to. He said he'd check in regularly for follow-ups. Then he handed me scripts for Xanax and Inderal and wished me a good day.

That was it. Two goddamned scripts. So much for his promise years earlier: We'll do some observations, run tests, ask questions, and at the end of three months you'll have a diagnosis and a treatment plan. I'd had a blood draw and initial psych tests. His questions led only to false confessions and broken promises. I was still scared—and in worse shape than when I walked into Rush.

I would see Bobbi twice a week as a hospital outpatient and once a week on Saturdays at her private office. If I stayed "stable," we'd cut back the hospital visits and keep Saturdays. *If* was a huge, scary word.

Before dawn on my last morning, I lay in the dim room, feeling the horror and the countless memories press in. This room had been my safe place and my prison. I wondered if the next person in the tiny bed would know what awaited her. Poor soul. Probably not.

I pulled my gum chain off the wall. Early on, Bobbi showed me how to fold wrappers into links. Like an inmate, I used a link a day to mark captivity. The chain now read 1,466.

I dressed Baby in her overalls and slipped into my too-big jeans, then waited for the discharge papers. I waited through 8 a.m. breakfast and 9 a.m. meds, half fearing it was a farce, and I wasn't going anywhere.

This one wasn't. A knock at the door. "I'm Sandy from the business office with your papers. You're free to leave."

Free. I had no idea what that would entail, but after being watched twenty-four hours a day, seven days a week, I'd take it.

On a Saturday morning in September, four years and six days after I arrived, I walked through the open steel door with Baby in one arm and my discharge papers and car keys in the other. I waited to hear it clang shut—to know the days of making up stories to keep my sanity were finally over.

"Well, Baby," I said, buckling her into the passenger seat. "I guess it's just you and me."

"Me, too?" I heard as I started the car. "Me woves you, Damie."

I took a deep breath. "Yes, Becky. Of course I love you, too. Let's go home and see if we can make a life together."

# The Rest of the Story

Starting over wasn't as easy as I thought it would be. Nothing felt the same once I left home. I was a 43-year-old divorcée with a new name, who had spent four years in a psych ward. My records said I was sometimes suicidal or homicidal and had been involved in a satanic cult that sacrificed babies. I had a half-empty apartment, no job, and no friends—but I had Bobbi.

After I dropped off my suitcase and Baby at my new apartment, I drove to Bobbi's private office, where I would continue toxic "therapy" every other Saturday. We were codependent. Each of us had our reasons for needing the other.

Continuing therapy with Bobbi was a mistake. Money was tight—I still needed basic household items—but I agreed to pay her more than I could afford. At first, we sat together on her cream-colored leather couch and talked about how hard it was to return to daily life. Then, for months, we discussed what I wanted to do for a living. Like in the hospital, there was no real therapy— no exploration of my psyche or trauma. It was more like chatting with a friend about how to cope with life.

One day in session, I mentioned wanting to visit my mother, who had suffered a stroke. As "my friend," Bobbi offered to go with me, and I was glad she did. Mom didn't recognize me at first.

She told the nurse her daughter was dead, which was hard to hear. Bobbi held my hand and asked if I wanted to leave, and I almost did. But just as I was about to go, Mom looked at me, gave a crooked smile, and asked me to sit beside her. We reminisced about the old neighborhood, dance school, and the costumes she had made for me and my best friend, June. I was about to ask if she saw my brothers when, abruptly, she said, "Time to eat." She then got up and walked toward the dining area. I wasn't surprised. Food had always been her comfort.

The nurse asked me not to visit again because any disruption to her routine caused her to become mean, hit people, and grow uncontrollable. I was also told she never opened any cards or letters.

I asked if I would be notified when she passed and was told yes. But the notification arrived a week late. Once again, I had no closure. Both my mother and father died without a formal goodbye, which still haunts me.

But there was always the other Bobbi—the doctor, therapist Bobbi—who I sensed kept me around to reinforce the lie that I was a ritual abuse survivor. She often slipped in reminders that I'd be safer if I didn't tell anyone what I'd been through.

Despite the damage, I managed to rebuild parts of my life. I returned to college and earned a master's degree in library science. Eventually, I moved from my apartment into a condo.

I tried relationships with both men and women but couldn't commit until I understood why genuine love frightened me so deeply. Hurting someone again—like I had hurt Dave—was something I couldn't risk.

From the outside, I looked fine. I smiled, joined a choir, got along with neighbors. But it was a façade. Inside, I was constantly on guard—hypervigilant, always scanning for danger. In the summer heat, I'd struggle with sexual compulsions I didn't understand.

Those compulsions—unlabeled, undiagnosed—followed me for decades. After another humiliating episode, I tried traditional therapy, but the fear of being drugged and controlled again, along with Bobbi's rule of silence, kept me guarded. Over time, the urges lessened, and I made peace with never fully understanding why they began.

When I lost faith in traditional medicine, I turned to alternative paths. I spent thousands on psychics, astrologers, and a man who claimed to read the Akashic Records. None had answers. Eventually, I turned to Native American spirituality and completed four vision quests under the guidance of a Lakota teacher.

Each year for four years, I spent twenty-four hours alone on remote land with no food or water, wearing only a cotton dress and carrying two blankets and a handmade pipe. I prayed for understanding—but Tunkashila, the Great Spirit, remained silent.

How could I find the truth when I didn't even know where to look? I thought the women at Rush were the only ones accused of horrific acts. I had no idea I was part of a nationwide hysteria— the satanic panic. There was no Google then, and even if there had been, I wouldn't have known what to search for.

Still, part of me had never believed I was a cult survivor. That flicker of doubt stayed alive. One day, Bobbi told me she and Braun were being sued by two women from Rush. They wanted me to join the suit as a witness to the unethical treatment we'd endured. Bobbi insisted she'd done nothing wrong and that her assets were protected. I could've joined them—but I was still under her spell. I didn't.

The suit was settled out of court. Both plaintiffs received millions. If I had joined them, my life might have changed. Not just financially—emotionally. I would have been validated years sooner.

It wasn't until October 1998 that my truth cracked open. I was watching *Dateline*, my favorite show, when the headline appeared: *"Devil's Advocate?"* Then came the names: *Dr. Braun. Rush.*

My stomach dropped. I could barely breathe.

Millions watched as Braun tried to justify his false diagnoses.

That smug, dismissive smirk—the same one I'd seen for years—made me want to destroy everything in sight. What I had suspected all along was true. We'd been sold out for money, prestige, and power.

As I sat frozen, something shifted inside me. For the first time, I felt permission to speak.

That night, I began to accept that I—and many others—had been victims not of satanic abuse, but of medical abuse. I finally understood that Bobbi had been wrong. Part of me wanted to confront her, but she had already closed her practice and disappeared out of state.

My outrage burned. I needed to talk. I needed to tell the truth. I returned to therapy—real therapy.

It took months to build trust and unpack the lies, guilt, and shame I'd carried. Becky still surfaced sometimes—her role as protector forged in hypnosis and drugs. She didn't vanish. She lingered, ready to stick out her tongue whenever I felt fear.

Anger still rises when I hear about the mistreatment of psychiatric patients. But more often now, there's acceptance. I've learned that wherever I am is where I'm meant to be—whether I'm writing about my life, making dinner, or visiting the memory unit in the facility where I live.

During the five years it took to write this memoir, both Braun and Bobbi died. Their deaths brought an unexpected peace.

My thoughts still flit like butterflies, landing on what nourishes me, darting away when I'm triggered. I still feel red-hot anger at injustice. But mostly, I've accepted that I am where I'm supposed to be.

Today, I live in a retirement community of 450 people, with five levels of care. I still count objects, repeat phrases, and get anxious when things are out of order. But I feel safe here.

The memory residents—the lost ones who mix words and wander halls—are my favorites. Their nonsensical chatter touches my soul because I've been there too: living inside confusion, trying to remember who I was and what was real.

My confusion came from drugs and unethical therapy. Theirs from fading memory. But suffering recognizes suffering. I can meet them where they are, even if just for a moment.

This is where I stand now. I don't have a "happily ever after." I'm not healed—not entirely. I still slip into the "good girl" who tries to please. My life isn't what I hoped it would be—but it isn't over.

And so, I leave this story unfinished. Because I have no idea what's waiting for me, just around the corner.

# Timeline - Bennett G. Braun

1963: Braun graduated from Tulane University with a bachelor's degree in psychology and he earned a master's in the same subject in 1964.

1968: Braun earned his medical degree from the University of Illinois in 1968.

1968-69: He interned at Michael Reese Medical Center.

1969-71: He did his residency at the University of Chicago hospitals.

1982-84: Braun did another residency at Rush University Medical Center.

1984: He published articles and opened the Dissociative Disorders Unit at Rush. He started holding conferences.

1984-1985: Braun co-founded the International Society for the Study of Multiple Personality. This organization contributed to the spread of satanic panic. It's still in existence today, but changed its name to the International Society for the Study of Trauma and Dissociation.

1985: I was admitted to his unit.

1986: Patricia Burgus was admitted and was my roommate for one week.

1986: Elizabeth Gale was admitted.

1988: Geraldo Rivera hosted an episode of Dateline titled "Devil Worship: Exposing Satan's Underground." This documentary helped spread fear around the world.

1989: I was discharged from Rush.

1993 - Patricia Burgus filed a lawsuit against Braun and Sachs. This case had tremendous news coverage and would end without going to trial.

1994: Braun received an award for his "services to women" from Gloria Steinem.

1995: Geraldo Rivera apologized for his 1988 show.

1997: Patricia Burgus was awarded $10.6 million. It was considered one of the largest settlements in a "false memory" or "recovered memory" lawsuit and is often cited as a landmark case in the end of the "satanic panic" therapeutic era.

1998: Braun's unit was shuttered, likely due to his inability to obtain sufficient malpractice insurance.

1998: The NBC *Dateline* program *Devil's Advocate* #787 aired on October 27. This was released around the time the Burgus case was making headlines.

1998: Braun and Roberta G. Sachs were named as unindicted co-conspirators in the first criminal trial of USA v. Peterson et al. It ended in a mistrial.

1999: Braun's license was suspended for two years due to the Burgus suit. There were eight counts of wrongdoing. Under each count, there was a minimum of 45 allegations. After the suspension, he faced a minimum 5-year probation period that precluded him from treating patients diagnosed with multiple personality disorder or dissociative identity disorder. Braun admitted no wrongdoing.

2001: Braun took an administrative job at Helena, Montana's Shodair Hospital.

2002: Elizabeth Gale sued.

2003: Braun obtained a license in Montana, a state that does not require doctors to have malpractice insurance coverage. After obtaining a Montana license, Braun opened a private practice.

2004: Gale settled for $7.5 million. She had come to believe she was a breeder for Satan and gave birth to babies that were then sacrificed. Her case was settled before depositions were taken.
2016: Braun partially retired, reducing his patient load from around 240 to around 30 patients, and began seeing his patients in his home.
2017: The Drug Enforcement Agency investigated Braun, prompting him to surrender his controlled substance prescribing privileges that same year.
2018: Braun renewed his medical license. He disclosed in that application he had voluntarily relinquished his DEA-controlled substance prescription authorization. He admitted no wrongdoing.
2019: Ciara Rehbein sued him for overprescribing medication that left her with a permanent facial tic. She also filed a complaint against the Montana Board of Medical Examiners for allowing him a license, despite knowing his past.
2020: Because of the Rehbein case, Braun lost his Montana license to practice medicine. He was prohibited from reapplying.
2024: Braun died while on vacation in Florida after a fall.

# Timeline - Roberta (Bobbi) G. Sachs

1975: Sachs received a master of arts degree in education from Northwestern University.

1976: She received a doctorate in education from Northwestern University.

1982: Sachs was issued two Illinois licenses: one as a clinical psychologist and a second as a registered psychologist. Today, this likely wouldn't happen because a doctorate in psychology or equivalent is required, and the registered psychologist category has effectively vanished.

1985: Sachs joined the staff at Rush. She worked in a variety of roles, including director of training and assistant professor of psychology.

1985: I was admitted to Rush and first saw Sachs on September 6.

1993-99: The Patricia Burgus civil lawsuit was settled for $10.6 million, one of the highest ever in a false memory case. Both Dr. Bennett Braun and Sachs faced numerous charges.

1995-2000: Sachs was named in a series of medical malpractice suits filed by several former patients.

1998: Sachs moved to Maryland shortly before the *Dateline* program aired.

1999-2003: On behalf of John Doe, his family sued his health care team, which included Braun and Sachs. His suit alleged that the defendants diagnosed him with multiple personality disorder when he was underage. This case was settled for $5.25 million. Sachs' portion was just over $3 million.

2003: Sachs was reprimanded for failing to adequately document her treatment of a patient and for not questioning certain medication protocols. She paid a $5,000 fine and would never practice again as a psychologist. Her LinkedIn profile at the time said, "I have been a clinical psychologist working primarily with trauma for over 30 years. I am now working with adults who are on a spiritual path."

2004: Elizabeth Gale was awarded a $7.5 million settlement after suing Braun, Sachs, and Rush Medical Center for alleged false-memory and over-medication practices. Between 1988 and 1994, she had been hospitalized 18 times, for a total of 5 1/2 years.

2021: Sachs died on September 10. Her obituary in the Chicago Tribune erroneously said she had psychology degrees. It also said she "dedicated her life to helping the severely abused and was regarded as one of the leading experts in treating patients with multiple personality disorders."

While she was lauded as a hero by some, she contributed to destroying numerous lives and families. Braun was the mastermind, but Sachs was right there with him, publishing articles, speaking at conferences, and making videos to help therapists treat victims of satanic ritual abuse. Together, they made history and caused incalculable harm.

# Acknowledgements

First and foremost, I sincerely thank my book coach, Kim Curtis, who believed in me when I couldn't, supported me when I wanted to give up, and encouraged me to face my pain when I wasn't ready. She was the one steady presence who walked with me and helped me feel I had a life to reclaim.

To Parthenia Hicks, who encouraged me to express my thoughts more openly and pushed me to share more about my family life.

To my fellow writers in the St. Charles Writers' Group, who read my second draft and offered thoughtful suggestions for improvement, and to the group's leader, Lisa Macaione, who always told me, "You've got this."

To Lisa Heiman, who read an early draft and spent time in that same psychiatric ward during her troubled teen years.

To Nick Heath and Andrea Robertson, who, no matter how early it was or how busy they were, always took time to listen to me talk—or cry—as I worked through the many layers of deceit I had endured.

# About the Author

Jamie Lyn Weaver is a first-time author with a master's degree in library science.

In 2024, she received an honorable mention for the first chapter of this memoir at the prestigious San Miguel Writers' Conference & Literary Festival. After attending the conference, there was no stopping her. She was determined to tell her personal account of the intricacies and consequences of being kept in a locked psych ward during the satanic panic era.

Jamie lives surrounded by her favorite books in a retirement community in the northwest suburbs of Chicago.

Please visit Jamie's website, https://jamielynweaver.com, for contact info, book excerpts and other information.

# Resources

There are many excellent Wikipedia articles about the satanic panic era, and Dr. Braun's name appears in some of them. However, the following sources helped me most in understanding how genuinely complicated this movement was.

<u>Book</u>

Making Monsters: False Memories, Psychotherapy, and Sexual Hysteria by Richard Ofshe and Ethan Watters (https://amzn.to/4b1H2T8)

<u>YouTube</u>

"Influence in Psychotherapy: The Big Picture" — Richard Ofshe, December 1994 (https://bit.ly/47eNqoT)

"The Memory Wars" — Matt Orchard, July 2021 (https://bit.ly/4m9xURC)

<u>Guest Essay</u>

"The Forgotten Lessons of the Recovered Memory Movement" *The New York Times* (2022) — Ethan Watters (https://nyti.ms/4aV4nG8)

<u>Websites</u>

False Memory Syndrome Foundation: This was the main website I referred to during my research. It has extensive archives and searchable tabs, including *Families, Questioning Memories,* and *General Information.* A registration form must be completed before access is granted. (http://www.fmsfonline.org/)

Grey Faction: This website also provides resources like those of the False Memory Syndrome Foundation. Its pages describe who they are, what they stand for, and include a helpful therapist-license lookup tool organized by state. (https://greyfaction.org/)

<u>Facebook</u>

False Memory Syndrome Action Network: This private Facebook group is for anyone who has either been accused of false memories or has a friend or family member who has been wrongfully accused. It was especially helpful to me, as it allowed me to connect with others who had been at Rush as well as at other institutions. (https://bit.ly/3OS2Edd)

It was through this group that I learned those who had been falsely accused call themselves *retractors,* because they retracted everything they had been coerced to confess.

Today, I continue to read many entries from families devastated by false accusations of sexual abuse by a parent or sibling. This group remains a supportive community when doubts arise, and you feel you're alone.